THE PRACTITIONERS' GUIDE TO
TEACHING THINKING SERIES

EVALUATING
CRITICAL THINKING

D1478883

WRITTEN BY

Stephen P. Norris & Robert H. Ennis

SERIES EDITED BY

Robert J. Swartz & D. N. Perkins

SERIES TITLES

TEACHING THINKING: ISSUES AND APPROACHES
TECHNIQUES FOR TEACHING THINKING
EVALUATING CRITICAL THINKING

© 1989
**CRITICAL THINKING
PRESS & SOFTWARE**
(Formerly Midwest Publications)
P.O. Box 448 · Pacific Grove · CA 93950-0448
ISBN 89455-380-1

TABLE OF CONTENTS

FOREWARD

Teaching for thinking has become a major agenda in schools across this country. No one, of course, doubts that in the past educators have been concerned about the quality of student thinking and have worked to improve it. Such attempts, however, have all too often fallen prey to the pressures for coverage and for learning factual information with which all teachers have to cope. Today, by contrast, teachers in many schools are learning to manage—and even modify—the demands of coverage while emphasizing the development of forms of thinking that foster learning, understanding, and critical and creative thought. This shift reaffirms the value we place on good thinking. It also underscores the need not only to continue with these attempts but to turn more of them into greater successes. It is in this spirit that we offer a series of reflective guides for educational practitioners. We believe that enough is known today about thinking and how it can be taught to put into the hands of practitioners guide books that synthesize the relevant work of leaders in this field. This series presents a systematic conception of the aims of teaching for thinking and guidelines for achieving these aims in interactions with our students.

There is a second, less upbeat reason for publishing these volumes. Like any major shift in institutional priorities, the boom in efforts to explicitly teach thinking has provoked a wide variety of disparate approaches, claims, and advocates. They all tell us what we should be aiming at in teaching thinking and how best to do it. Often, however, hidden beneath the use of more or less the same terminology are quite different goals and means. While there is a sense in which such a ferment is healthy in a young field, the danger of fadism, miscommunication, and superficiality looms large, especially when there are pressures for immediate change and publishers are eager to respond.

It is our conviction that good thinking can be taught as a normal and comfortable element of educational practice. However, this mission cannot be accomplished overnight. It requires the very same good thinking and good sense that we all espouse as goals for our students. Thus, there is a need to stand back from the details of different methodologies and develop a broader perspective in which we tolerate a multiplicity of approaches while at the same time acknowledging a common basis lodged in a clear concept of good thinking and in a set of sound principles for teaching thinking that virtually all well-founded efforts should reflect.

We have created this series as a context in which these common goals and principles can be set out in order to provide practiced guidance to the classroom teacher and school administrator. They are the ones who have to make choices about how to implement the goal of developing students' thinking. But they do not have the time to probe the research in detail or travel around the country familiarizing themselves with approaches that claim success. Where there are basic alternatives for the teacher set against this common backdrop, these are spelled out and their scope and limits clarified.

The original concept for this series developed out of the first in a succession of annual faculty seminars sponsored and supported by the Critical and Creative Thinking Program at the University of Massachusetts at Boston, held in the summer of 1985. The participants in the seminar were:

Joan Baron	Conn. State Department of Education
Rebecca van der Bogert	Groton (MA) School System
Arthur Costa	Sacramento (CA) State University
Robert Ennis	University of Illinois
Bena Kallick	Weston Woods Foundation
Arthur Millman	University of Mass. at Boston
Stephen Norris	Memorial University of Newfoundland

Richard Paul	Sonoma State (CA) University
David Perkins	Harvard University
Linda Phillips	Memorial University of Newfoundland
Stephen Schwartz	University of Mass. at Boston
Alma Swartz	Westford (MA) School System
Robert Swartz	University of Mass. at Boston
S. Lee Winocur	Costa Mesa (CA) School District
Mary Anne Wolff	North Reading (MA) School System

While the ideas developed in these books are the authors' own, their root source and the motivation for the volumes derive from this seminar. We thank all the participants for their contributions to the development of each of these volumes. We are all dedicated to making good teaching of good thinking happen in our schools and to promoting the use of the very same good thinking on the part of professional educators as they plan and carry out this teaching.

ROBERT J. SWARTZ, FOUNDER
CRITICAL AND CREATIVE THINKING PROGRAM
UNIVERSITY OF MASSACHUSETTS AT BOSTON, AND

D. N. PERKINS, CO-DIRECTOR
PROJECT ZERO
HARVARD UNIVERSITY

GENERAL EDITORS

EDITORS' PREFACE

How can we tell how well students are thinking critically? How can we tell whether the programs and projects we are undertaking to teach critical thinking are having an impact? In their book, *Evaluating Critical Thinking*, Professors Stephen Norris and Robert Ennis provide us with answers to these questions.

Many books on evaluation are written for researchers or technicians. Such books often presume that what is being evaluated involves a broad set of practices in which many individuals participate and that the results are to be communicated to the public.

Evaluating Critical Thinking does address questions about how such evaluations of efforts to teach critical thinking should be conducted. But this volume is *also* refreshingly written to speak to the needs of practitioners in the field who have specifically classroom and school-based concerns. The classroom teacher often wants to know how well students already do critical thinking so that lessons can be constructed at the right level. He or she also wants to know if students are grasping the essentials of critical thinking. Formal evaluations are often not feasible or appropriate in these contexts. What other less formal information can such teachers gather to make reliable judgments of this sort? Professors Norris and Ennis provide significant guidance to practitioners who have these concerns.

Evaluating Critical Thinking is the third volume in our series of guidebooks for practitioners of teaching thinking, and it elaborates ideas introduced in the first volume, *Teaching Thinking: Issues and Approaches*. However, this book also introduces many new ideas related to assessing critical thinking not covered in that volume. It is a natural follow-up to the second volume, *Classroom Techniques in Teaching Thinking,* by Professors Arthur Costa and Lawrence Lowery. It provides a useful guide for those concerned about assessment who teach critical thinking infused into regular subject-area instruction or who teach it in separate courses.

This book establishes the context for evaluating critical thinking by first analyzing what we should look for in good critical thinkers. The conception of critical thinking that is spelled out in this analysis is one we share. It involves the active and appropriate use of key critical-thinking skills in judging the reasonableness of ideas and the justification of actions, set in the context of attitudes and dispositions that place value on careful and open thinking. In critical thinking, so construed, we search for good reasons that aid us in making decisions. Professors Norris and Ennis feel as we do: that, as humans, we do such thinking more or less well, but that we can be taught how to improve. The effectiveness of such teaching can be maximized if it pervades everything we do as educators.

It is here that the need arises to determine how well students are improving their thinking. Are the curricular efforts described in the first two volumes in this series worth implementing? What impact *do* they have on students' thinking?

This creates a challenge for anyone committed to teaching and evaluating critical thinking. Such assessments must show a *combination* of factors present in an individual as he or she thinks through issues while using a body of varied content knowledge both in school and outside the classroom. Different skills must be in use, as appropriate, and the person using them should display a variety of character traits and dispositions that capture what many have called a "critical spirit." How can we gather information about this multiplicity of factors?

The scope and limits of using available multiple-choice tests to gather information about these factors is reviewed by Professors Norris and Ennis. Also, they make suggestions about how, within the constraints of what you can and cannot learn from such tests, you can make your own state-of-the-art multiple-choice test. In addition, a rich variety of other types of tests, including essay tests and various sorts of short-answer tests, are also discussed.

They offer advice to the reader about how to construct and score these and ways that writing can be used in general as an indicator of the quality of critical thinking.

Finally, the authors discuss more challenging forms of qualitative assessment and provide very helpful practical suggestions for the classroom teacher. They explain how we can use interviews with students and, especially, how classroom observation can provide us with important and reliable information. They suggest various record-keeping techniques that teachers can master easily—e.g., keeping focused journals. *All* of these are important assessment tools.

Like the other volumes in this series, this book is dedicated to the idea that—as professionals—teachers and school administrators can and should exercise their own good thinking in making wise choices of the tools and techniques that they use. We are proud to include in this series a volume on assessment that is so accessible and provides such a valuable framework for practitioners to use in making these choices.

ROBERT J. SWARTZ AND D. N. PERKINS
SERIES EDITORS

AUTHORS' PREFACE

This book is aimed at a broad audience of people who have an interest in evaluating critical thinking: classroom teachers, school administrators, curriculum specialists, and evaluators. The book contains sections that are of specific interest to each of these groups, but every section should be of some interest to all readers.

The first requirement for any successful evaluation is having a defensible conception of critical thinking. Thus, the opening chapter asks and attempts to provide a somewhat detailed answer for the question, "What is critical thinking?" Another essential ingredient for a successful evaluation is that its purpose be clear. Evaluations of critical thinking can have different purposes and, depending upon the purpose, can proceed in different directions. Chapters 4 and 6 deal with some possible reasons why critical thinking might be evaluated and examine elements common to each of these purposes. Since one element common to all evaluations is that decisions must be made about the relative value of things, we urge that value judgments cannot be avoided.

Evaluations of critical thinking, whatever their purpose, rely upon gathering quality information on students' critical thinking. Chapters 2 to 5 deal with judging the quality of information, choosing and using commercially available critical thinking tests, constructing high quality multiple-choice tests for measuring certain aspects of critical thinking, and designing open-ended approaches for gathering quality information on students' critical thinking. Throughout these chapters a recurrent idea is that judgments of quality should take into account the use or uses to which the information on students' critical thinking will be put.

Gathering quality information is not sufficient, if that information is not used properly. Chapter 6 deals briefly with cautions that must be exercised in drawing conclusions from information gathered on students' critical thinking, be those conclusions about the students themselves, teachers, critical thinking programs, schools, or school districts. Essentially, we urge that the interpretation of information on students' critical thinking requires the use of critical thought!

We have arranged the chapters in what seems like a logical order to us, but the order may not suit everyone. Broadly speaking, chapters 1, 2, and 6 are more theoretical than the others. Those who are most concerned with practical advice on choosing and constructing tests may wish to begin reading with chapter 3 and proceed to 4 and 5. If this is your preference, we make one suggestion: at least read first the section in chapter 1 called "A Definition of Critical Thinking." You may also find if you begin reading with chapter 3 that there are several terms which you do not understand. Many of these are introduced in chapter 2, so you may refer to that chapter or to the glossary.

One of the messages of this book is that critical thinking evaluation is not an easy task. There is no precise formula or set of rules that can mechanically generate a good evaluation. As we conclude in the last chapter, the most important principle to follow is that the evaluation be guided by the standards of critical thought.

ACKNOWLEDGEMENTS

Aspects of this work result from research which Stephen Norris conducted under grants from the Social Sciences and Humanities Research Council of Canada: Grant Numbers 418-81-0781, 410-83-0697, and 410-85-0587. However, the views expressed herein are not necessarily those of the granting agency.

Stephen Norris thanks Memorial University of Newfoundland for granting him a sabbatical leave, during which the book was completed, and the Center for the Study of Reading, University of Illinois at Urbana-Champaign, where the leave was spent and whose facilities were used during the final writing.

Robert Ennis thanks the Spencer Foundation and the Center for Advanced Study in the Behavioral Sciences for their generous support while he developed some of the ideas in this book.

They both thank Linda Phillips and Sean Ennis for their comments on earlier drafts, and Kevin O'Reilly and Linda Phillips for permission to use their materials.

STEPHEN P. NORRIS
ROBERT H. ENNIS

CHAPTER ONE

WHAT IS CRITICAL THINKING?

There are many questions to ask when contemplating the evaluation of students' critical thinking. What is the best way to gather information on critical thinking? Should we use existing critical thinking tests? How do we tell whether these tests are good? Are there other ways to evaluate critical thinking? Should critical thinking be evaluated outside of standard school subjects? How can an evaluation best be designed? Will the information that is gathered be suitable for the purposes of the evaluation? Why evaluate students' critical thinking in the first place?

All of the above questions are important, but none of them can be answered prior to responding to the question, "What is critical thinking?" If we do not know what we mean by critical thinking, we have no way to decide whether we should try to evaluate it, whether to use existing critical thinking tests, or whether these tests are any good.

In volume 1 in this series the authors noted that the term "critical thinking" is used in education in a variety of ways— sometimes to refer simply to thinking and other times to all of good thinking. These seem idiosyncratic uses. After considerable thought and investigation, we feel that the following basic definition comes closer to expressing the way the term is generally used in education: *Critical thinking is reasonable and reflective thinking that is focused upon deciding what to believe or do.* However, this simple one-sentence definition is not detailed enough to provide guidance for many evaluation decisions. Elaboration is needed, and we shall soon offer that.

To summarize, then, we start this book by addressing the question, "What is critical thinking?" because an answer to this question is presupposed in attempts to deal with other questions about evaluating critical thinking. We shall propose an answer in the first section of the chapter that can serve as a basis for evaluation decisions, but we shall not insist on our answer. We only insist that you must have a clear, defensible notion of critical thinking in order to deal with critical thinking evaluation. In the second section, however, we do offer an appraisal of our definition.

Before elaborating on our definition of critical thinking, we will provide an example of thinking, using a letter to the editor of a fictitious newspaper. The letter is adapted from The Ennis-Weir Critical Thinking Essay Test, which we will discuss in chapter 3. Throughout this chapter we will often refer to the letter to illustrate points.

Example of Thinking

In the letter below a person is considering whether overnight parking should be prohibited on Moorburg's streets between 2 a.m. and 6 a.m. We will not evaluate the thinking now by saying it is critical or uncritical, good or poor. However, we will address such qualifications throughout the chapter.

Dear Editor:

Overnight parking on all streets in Moorburg should be eliminated. To achieve this goal, parking should be prohibited from 2 a.m. to 6 a.m. There are a number of reasons why any intelligent citizen should agree.

Three important streets, Lincoln Avenue, Marquand Avenue, and West Main Street, are very narrow. With cars parked on the streets, there really isn't room for the heavy traffic that passes over them in the afternoon rush hour. When driving home in the afternoon after work, it takes me thirty-five minutes to make a trip that takes ten minutes during the uncrowded time. If there were no cars parked on the side of these streets, they could handle considerably more traffic.

The opponents of my suggestions have said that conditions are safe enough now. These people don't know what "safe" really means. Conditions are not safe if there's even the slightest possible chance for an accident. That's what "safe" means. So, conditions are not safe the way they are now.

Finally, let me point out that the Director of the National Traffic Safety Council, Kenneth O. Taylor, has strongly recommended that overnight street parking be prevented on busy streets in cities the size of Moorburg. The National Association of Police Chiefs has made the same recommendation. Both suggest that prohibiting parking from 2 a.m. to 6 a.m. is the best way to prevent overnight parking. Sincerely,

Robert R. Raywift

Section One: A Definition of Critical Thinking

In this section we will first discuss the precise, one-sentence definition of critical thinking stated above. This definition provides the central idea of critical thinking. From this point, we will give a comprehensive overview of the process of critical thinking, based upon a pictorial representation. Then, we will offer a detailed account of the factors involved in the critical thinking process, and, finally, discuss how critical thinking as we conceive it relates to creative thinking and to good thinking generally.

>> *The central idea*

Critical thinking is reasonable and reflective thinking that is focused upon deciding what to believe or do. This sentence contains a lot of information and several key words. Let us examine it in more detail.

First, critical thinking is defined as *reasonable* thinking. This means that it is good thinking that relies appropriately upon the use of good reasons. People who form beliefs or who act without good reasons are acting arbitrarily and unreasonably. Good thinking is not arbitrary, however, because good thinking does not lead to just *any* conclusions, but in general to the *best* conclusions. The best conclusions are those supported by the best reasons, so critical thinking must rely upon good reasons in reaching conclusions. In his letter, Raywift relied upon reasons. Are all his reasons good, however, and, if not, which ones are poor and why are they poor?

Our detailed account of critical thinking abilities and dispositions discussed later in this section provides a way to answer these questions. For now, we can point out that he is arguing that parking be prohibited from 2 a.m. to 6 a.m., but his reason in the second paragraph of the letter refers to the need to relieve traffic congestion during the afternoon rush hour. Relieving congestion at that time cannot be a good reason for prohibiting overnight street parking, so that portion of his thinking is not reasonable. He has a reason, but it is not a *good* reason.

Second, critical thinking is defined as *reflective* thinking. Critical thinkers must be reflective in that they examine the reasonableness of their own and others' thought. Thinking does not become reasonable thinking by accident. Critical thinkers must *consciously* seek and use good reasons. Saying that critical thinking is reflective thinking is meant to indicate this overt, conscious aspect of good thinking. Was Raywift reflective in his letter writing? We cannot know for sure because we have not witnessed his actions. However, it does appear that he was at least somewhat reflective.

Third, critical thinking is *focused* thinking. This attribute is closely related to the previous one because it, too, suggests that critical thinking is consciously directed. To say that an activity is consciously directed is to say that it has a purpose. Critical thinking is purposeful thinking as it does not occur accidently or without reason. Raywift's thinking was focused, it appears. Note, however, that being focused is not enough; reasonableness and reflectiveness are also needed.

Fourth, the focus of critical thinking is a *decision about what to believe or do*. This characteristic indicates that critical thinking can evaluate statements (what we believe) and actions (what we do). Deciding what statements to believe has sometimes been considered the main concern of critical thinking. However, limiting critical thinking to the believability of statements is considered by some (we think rightly) to be impractical. Including in the definition a focus on decisions about *action* is intended to highlight the practical role that critical thinking can play in our lives. Raywift's focus was a decision about action—the action of prohibiting overnight street parking in Moorburg. Taken together, decisions about beliefs and actions comprise all the decisions we can make.

This definition of critical thinking emphasizes the process of thinking, in harmony with the traditional goals of critical thinking instruction, which are concerned more with teaching *how* to think than with teaching *what* to think. The process is reasonable, reflective, and focused.

Although critical thinking is a process, it is a process used to deal with some content. This content might be part of a school subject, or of a situation or problem in everyday life.

We want to evaluate students' critical thinking with both sorts of content. We want to evaluate critical thinking within school subject matter, because thinking critically in a subject is an essential part of mastering it. We want to evaluate critical thinking within the context of everyday life, because thinking critically in everyday life is important to success and survival. This need for critical thinking in everyday life is a large part of the practical justification for teaching critical thinking. There is no basis for assuming that critical thinking instruction in school subjects will automatically transfer to everyday life, so critical thinking must sometimes be evaluated in everyday-life contexts.

In order to simplify our discussions, we will frequently consider critical thinking in the abstract, realizing that there always is some content involved in the actual doing of critical thinking. This abstract treatment is possible because there is much in common among the various content areas in which people should think critically. Further discussion of transfer and teaching for transfer is included in volume 1 of this series.

>> *A pictorial representation*

Critical thinking is a process focused on deciding what to believe or do. To make a decision, we rely upon some information, background knowledge, and previously accepted conclusions. These form the *basic support* for the decision. The link between

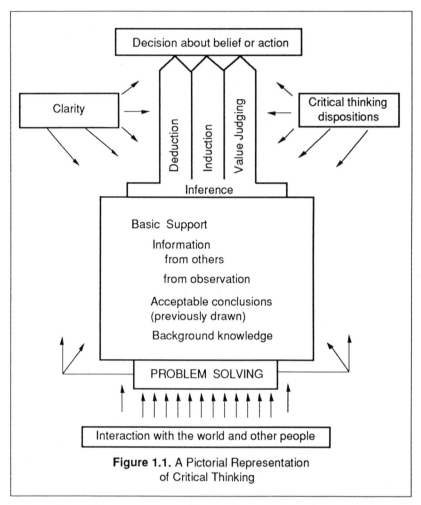

Figure 1.1. A Pictorial Representation
of Critical Thinking

the basis for the decision and the decision itself is the process of *inference*. We will therefore say at times that the decision is inferred from the starting information, background knowledge, and previously accepted conclusions.

The critical thinking process is represented in figure 1.1. The figure implies a direction from bottom to top. However, this does not mean that critical thinking follows an ordered, linear path. Figure 1.1 depicts the *logical* relationships involved, not how one thinks critically in practice. In practice, critical thinking can proceed in many directions and can stop, restart, and retrace.

The process is viewed broadly as part of problem solving, which is indicated by the Problem Solving box near the bottom of the figure. The process ends in a decision about belief or action indicated by the Decision box at the top of the figure. The Interaction box at the bottom of the figure shows that the whole process of reaching a decision usually rests in a context of interaction with the world and other people. The Basic Support box depicts the starting point of critical thinking, which consists of information from others and observation, previously accepted conclusions, and background knowledge. The Inference columns, indicating three basic types of inference, depict the logical step from the basic support to the final decision. The points on the columns indicate the direction of the logical inference. The Disposition box and the arrows coming from it depict the need to diffuse critical thinking dispositions throughout the whole critical thinking process. Finally, the Clarity box and the arrows emanating from it show how a concern with clarity must permeate the process of critical thinking.

Figure 1.1 can represent the logic of Raywift's thinking. He was trying to solve a problem and was interacting with other people in so doing. His thinking was directed towards a decision about an action (banning overnight street parking); it was based upon information from others and from his own observation; and it displayed inferences from the basic support he offered to his decision. Of course, there are problems with Raywift's thinking, as we have already indicated, so not all of it is critical thinking. For instance, not all of his inferences were sound, since he inferred that relief of afternoon rush-hour congestion is a reason for prohibiting overnight street parking. However, some of his thinking is critical thinking. For instance, he properly infers from the statements of legitimate authorities (assuming that they are legitimate authorities) in the area of traffic control. Their statements tend to support Raywift's view that overnight street parking should be prohibited, although Raywift did not mention that the authorities were referring only to busy streets.

>> *Abilities and dispositions*

In order to carry out the critical thinking process effectively, one needs both abilities and dispositions. The abilities include those required to interact effectively with other people, to judge the soundness of information and inferences drawn from information, to produce credible information and inferences, and to maintain clarity.

Since critical thinking takes place within a problem-solving context, and often in the context of interacting with other people, the critical thinker needs to be able to function effectively within these contexts. To do this, the person needs to employ certain strategies and tactics for keeping the problem-solving process on task, for communicating coherently with other people, and for dealing intelligibly with communication received from others.

To properly use information obtained from others and from observation as the basic support for decisions about belief or action, the critical thinker must be able to judge the soundness of this information. To serve as a sound basis of support for decisions, information should satisfy certain criteria of credibility. The critical thinker needs to know these criteria and be able to employ them properly in context. In addition, if the information comes from the person's own observations, the person must have the ability to observe well.

Since previously accepted conclusions also serve as the basis for decisions, critical thinkers must be able to assess these conclusions. Conclusions are reached through the process of inference, so the critical thinker must be able to judge the soundness of inferences. Inferences, too, are subject to certain criteria of appraisal, and the critical thinker must know these criteria and how to use them.

Besides being able to judge already-made inferences, the person must be able to make good inferences. Judging already-made inferences requires *evaluative* abilities as we discussed above. Making good inferences requires *productive* abilities. These include the ability to formulate candidate hypotheses that might meet the evaluative criteria used to judge inferences. The productive aspects of critical thinking indicate an overlap with creative thinking. We will discuss the relationship between critical and creative thinking later in this chapter.

Since the critical thinking process is to be permeated with clarity, the critical thinker must have the ability to maintain clarity. It must be clear, for example, which questions are being asked; what the information used as basic support means; what assumptions are being made; and what decision is being reached. The critical thinker must have the ability to sustain clarity at these points and many more.

The categories of abilities mentioned above are not sufficient for defining critical thinking. A person may have all the abilities but, for some reason, not use them. Therefore, in addition to possessing critical thinking abilities, critical thinkers must have the attitude and tendency to use the abilities they possess. Furthermore, attitudes are required for the person to be in the right frame of mind for thinking critically. Thinking critically is an activity which requires sustained effort and, therefore, certain commitments. One of the most important of these is a commitment to open-mindedness. For simplicity in this book, we will use the single term "disposition" to refer to attitudes, commitments, and tendencies to act.

>> *Interim summary*

We have described critical thinking as a process of reasonably and reflectively deciding what to believe or do. We depicted it as having three major parts. The final outcome is the decision about belief or action. This decision rests on some basic, supportive information. The third part is the logical link between the decision and the supportive information. This link is an inference.

In order for the critical thinking process to proceed, a person needs certain abilities and dispositions. The abilities can be grouped into four general sets:

- those involved in thinking clearly;
- those involved in making and evaluating inferences;
- those needed to establish a sound basis for inference;
- those involved in carrying out the critical thinking process in an orderly and effective way.

One must also be disposed to use the critical thinking abilities one possesses, and to maintain open-mindedness.

With this overview of critical thinking in place, we can offer a detailed specification of the critical thinking abilities and dispositions mentioned above. Although we will provide considerable detail, there is still more that could be said. For example, under the heading, "Clarity-related Abilities," we will refer to the ability to identify unstated reasons. This ability alone is quite involved, and more could be said about it than we will say about critical thinking in general. However, in this book we must stop far short of giving a complete picture. For further information we refer you to the suggested readings at the end of this chapter and to the other volumes in this series.

>> *Detailed definition*

The details of the abilities and dispositions which define critical thinking are provided in tables 1.1 and 1.2 in this chapter and in the appendix. Table 1.1 provides a list of critical thinking dispositions; table 1.2 gives a brief overview of critical thinking abilities; and the appendix provides the detailed breakdown of critical thinking abilities often needed when designing evaluations.

Taken together, the tables contain detailed outlines of the topics which might be covered in a critical thinking course or in teaching critical thinking in the context of specific school subjects. Therefore, they provide specifications for the content that can be covered in critical thinking evaluations. The tables do not include suggestions for appropriate levels of treatment at different grade levels; for sequencing material for instruction or evaluation; or for the relative emphasis to be placed on the various parts of the outline. In general, these issues must be addressed and resolved, taking into account the context of the evaluation, a topic which will be addressed at various points in chapters 4, 5, and 6. Issues of sequencing and emphasis are also examined in volume 1 of the series.

Table 1.1 contains a set of dispositions which define the *critical spirit*. The critical spirit is what motivates critical thinkers to apply critical thinking abilities to their own thinking and to that of others, and to want their own thinking to meet the standards of critical thought. The critical spirit motivates critical thinkers to hope that if their thought does not meet these standards, they will either recognize this fact themselves or that it will be pointed out to them. Broadly speaking, having the critical spirit makes the critical thinker a person with a certain type of character. Probably the most important element of this character is open-mindedness.

You might try to determine how well Raywift displayed critical thinking dispositions. Consider the disposition to use credible sources and mention them. Did Raywift do this? What qualifications would you make in your answer? Did Raywift try to keep his thinking relevant to the main point? Were there places where he did and other places where he did not?

Table 1.2 gives a brief list of topics to be covered when evaluating clarity-related abilities, basic support-related abilities, inference-related abilities, and strategies and tactics for going about the critical thinking process in an orderly and effective way. There are two major subdivisions within clarity-related abilities— Elementary Clarification and Advanced Clarification. Elementary clarification abilities are used in providing focus for the critical thinking process, in analyzing lines of reasoning, and in seeking and providing clarification in general. Advanced clarification abilities are used to provide and evaluate definitions of terms and in identifying assumptions that are left implicit in lines of reasoning.

Table 1.1

Topics for Evaluating

Critical Thinking Dispositions

Critical thinkers
1. seek a statement of the thesis or question;
2. seek reasons;
3. try to be well informed;
4. use credible sources and mention them;
5. take into account the total situation;
6. keep their thinking relevant to the main point;
7. keep in mind the original or most basic concern;
8. look for alternatives;
9. are open-minded and
   a. seriously consider points of view other than their own;
   b. reason from starting points with which they disagree without letting the disagreement interfere with their reasoning;
   c. withhold judgment when the evidence and reasons are insufficient
10. take a position and change a position when the evidence and reasons are sufficient to do so;
11. seek as much precision as the subject permits;
12. deal in an orderly manner with the parts of a complex whole;
13. employ their critical thinking abilities;
14. are sensitive to the feelings, level of knowledge, and degree of sophistication of others.

The abilities needed for establishing a sound basis for inference include those used in judging the credibility of sources of information, and in making and judging the credibility of observations. Judging observations is a part of judging the credibility of information in general, because observations made by ourselves and others are one source of information. A sound basis also includes previously drawn acceptable conclusions and background knowledge.

The inference-related abilities pertain to the three types of inference pictured in figure 1.1: deducing, inducing, and value judging. The abilities include those needed both for producing inferences and for judging inferences that have been made. There is overlap between these latter two categories, since the criteria for judging inferences should also guide the inference-making process. This overlap is just one reflection of the broader notion that the various aspects of critical thinking cannot be separated easily from one another. They can be *discussed* separately, as we are doing here, but during an actual process of deciding what to do or believe, one must employ abilities from different categories.

The critical thinking process also requires effective interaction with others and takes place within the problem-solving context. These abilities consist of a set of strategies and tactics which provide order for the critical thinking process. We do not mean a rigid, sequential order. Critical thinking cannot be properly characterized in this way. Rather, the order is inherent in the application of all those strategies and tactics that are needed, allowing for the possibility that they might be used in different sequences with the same result.

Which critical thinking abilities did Raywift use in his letter writing? Which did he not use, but should have used? Consider abilities involved in judging the credibility of a source, in making and judging inductions, and in defining terms and judging definitions. Maybe there are others. Can you identify any?

This completes the outline of topics for evaluating critical thinking. It is clear that the number of topics is quite large. You may feel overwhelmed. However, it would be very difficult to include fewer topics and still provide a comprehensive overview of critical thinking abilities and dispositions. The size of the list reflects the breadth of the subject.

Table 1.2
Topics for Evaluating
Critical Thinking Abilities
(Abbreviated Version)

Elementary Clarification
  1. Focusing on a question
  2. Analyzing arguments
  3. Asking and answering questions
     that clarify and challenge

Basic Support
  4. Judging the credibility of a source
  5. Making and judging observations

Inference
  6. Making and judging deductions
  7. Making and judging inductions
  8. Making and judging value judgments

Advanced Clarification
  9. Defining terms and judging definitions
  10. Identifying assumptions

Strategies and Tactics
  11. Deciding on an action
  12. Interacting with others

You must also remember that the topical outline itself does not provide all the understanding needed for evaluation. For example, suppose we wish to evaluate the basic support-related abilities, topics 4 and 5 in the appendix. If we look at topic 4, Judging the credibility of a source, subtopic h, Careful habits, we will need information about the identity of the careful habits before knowledge of this ability can be evaluated. Unfortunately, in a book of this limited size, we cannot provide all the information needed for evaluating the abilities and dispositions included in the tables. However, the discussions in chapters 3, 4, and 5, where we illustrate different types of information-gathering techniques, will go into some detail about the particular topics. The examples will thus provide a flavor for what is needed for evaluating critical thinking abilities and dispositions. For even more information, we again refer you to the additional readings suggested at the end of the chapters.

Note also that the appendix contains only critical thinking abilities that apply in a variety of subjects and topics. It does not indicate which critical thinking abilities apply in a given subject, but most are applicable in most subjects. The ability to judge the credibility of a source is applicable in, e.g., history, economics, government, literature, music, home economics, biology, chemistry, physics, physical education, sociology, anthropology, education, consumer education, driver education, and sex education.

>> *Critical thinking, creative thinking, and good thinking*

In this section we answer a series of questions which were also addressed in volume 1 of this series: What is the difference between critical and creative thinking? Do critical and creative thinking overlap? Is all good thinking either critical or creative? As you will see, our answers to these questions are consistent with those given in volume 1. The distinctions we will draw are conceptual; in actual thinking, critical and creative thinking are usually both present and deeply interdependent, even more than our conceptualizations suggest. As you can already see, the ensuing discussions will be somewhat abstract, so some readers may wish to skip to the next section. However, many readers will find the discussions enlightening.

Critical thinking, as we have defined it, forms a large and important part of good thinking generally, but it is not all of good thinking. This relationship between good thinking generally and critical thinking is depicted in figure 1.2.

The larger circle in figure 1.2 represents all of good thinking. Critical thinking is represented by the smaller circle inside the larger one, depicting that all critical thinking is good thinking, but that there is good thinking that is not critical thinking. Critical thinking is good thinking that is *reasonable* and *reflective*. That is, when thinking critically, a person consciously and deliberately seeks and uses good reasons in deciding what to believe or do.

The critical thinking circle is divided into two parts: evaluative and nonevaluative. Producing, but not yet evaluating, alternative hypotheses to explain some phenomenon is an example of critical thinking that falls into the nonevaluative part. Evaluating

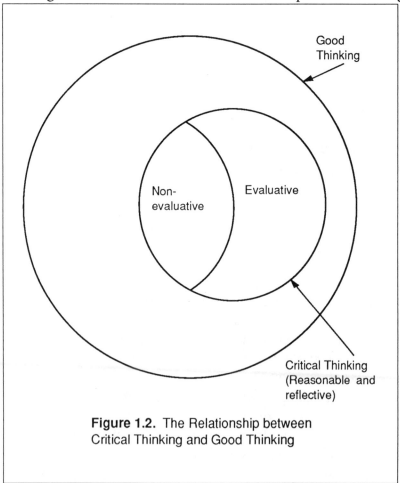

Figure 1.2. The Relationship between Critical Thinking and Good Thinking

those alternatives falls into the evaluative part. As we will presently show, the productive, nonevaluative aspects of critical thinking are where critical and creative thinking overlap.

Creative thinking is also a large and important part of good thinking in general. The relationship between creative thinking and good thinking is depicted in figure 1.3. Creative thinking is good thinking focused on original and effective products, that is, *reasonable* and *productive*. Producing possible alternative hypotheses to account for some phenomenon, writing a poem, or

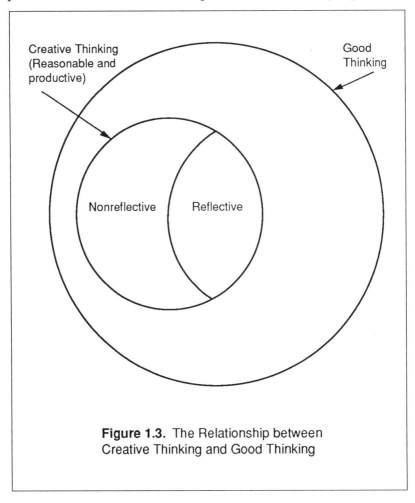

Figure 1.3. The Relationship between Creative Thinking and Good Thinking

composing a symphony are examples of creative thinking, if they
are of reasonably good quality.

The creative thinking circle is also divided into two parts:
reflective and nonreflective thinking. Both parts are needed. For
example, when explaining a phenomenon, a thinker may not
reflect while producing possible alternative hypotheses, but just
brainstorm reasonably. Alternatively, the thinker may consciously
and deliberately pose alternative hypotheses. Creative thinking
that is reflective overlaps with critical thinking, as we will presently show.

Creative thinking is never sufficient for deciding what
outcomes to accept. That is, it does not answer such questions as:
Which of the proposed hypotheses is the best explanation of the
phenomenon? Is the rhyme, meter, and imagery of the poem suitable for the intended message? Does the symphony display balance and contrast in an aesthetically pleasing manner? Creative
thinking requires evaluative critical thinking before its results can
be accepted.

Similarly, critical thinking often requires the support of creative thinking. For example, a hypothesis cannot be evaluated
with respect to competing hypotheses unless competitors have
been generated, and nonreflective creative thinking is often
required for that generation.

Figure 1.4 depicts the overlap between critical and creative
thinking. The circles for critical and creative thinking overlap and
lie completely inside the circle representing good thinking. The
overlapping area includes thinking that is *reasonable, productive, reflective,* but *nonevaluative.*

Remember that the figure depicts the *conceptual* relationships
involved. That is, it shows that critical and creative thinking are
somewhat different, but overlapping; that both critical and creative
thinking are completely included in good thinking; and that, even
when taken together, critical and creative thinking do not comprise
all of good thinking. The figure does not show, however, the in-

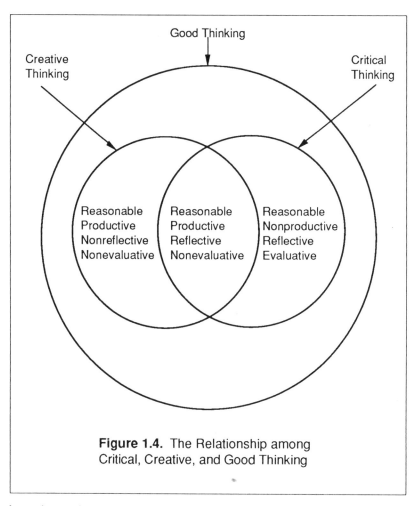

Figure 1.4. The Relationship among
Critical, Creative, and Good Thinking

interdependence of critical and creative thinking in real thinking situations. We believe they are very interdependent.

The circle for good thinking is larger than the overlapping combination of circles for critical and creative thinking; otherwise, the sizes of the circles have no significance. The circles for critical and creative thinking are the same size, but this should not be interpreted to mean that critical and creative thinking define equally large aspects of good thinking.We believe that critical and creative thinking form a very large part of good thinking, but we make no claims about the exact proportion or about the relative proportions of good thinking that are critical and creative. In addition, the degree of overlap between the circles for critical and creative thinking is not based on any claim about the actual degree of overlap which exists. We just do not know these things; nor does anyone else. Finally, our diagrams contain sharply defined boundaries between categories, but we believe that all the boundaries are fuzzy. Precision here would be unrealistic and misleading.

A few words are in order about good thinking that is neither critical nor creative. This type of thinking occurs frequently and indeed must occur if we are to get by in the world. Much of this good thinking is *automatized*, meaning that it occurs without conscious effort and reflection. For example, safely negotiating an automobile through busy city streets involves a considerable amount of automatic thinking. Evaluations are made about such things as speeds and distances of other cars. Such evaluations are often made automatically, so they do not have the reflective character of critical thinking. Nor do they have the productive character of creative thinking. Nevertheless, they are good thinking. Another example is the thinking used to follow a learned and well-practiced algorithm, such as the one for long division in arithmetic. All these sorts of thinking are contained in the area of the larger circle of figure 1.4 which is outside the critical thinking and creative thinking circles.

Section Two: Our Definition of Critical Thinking— An Appraisal

Since it is important to start with a defensible definition of critical thinking, let us sketch an appraisal of the definition we have offered.

>>   *Agreement among educators*

The basic, one-sentence definition finds a good consensus. Most theoreticians and practitioners believe that critical thinking is reflective, evaluative, and reasonable. Also, most educators prefer to think of critical thinking as serving both practical and academic needs. Our focus on decisions about belief and action allows for this dual concentration. Finally, most educators believe that critical thinking includes both abilities and dispositions, and our definition also includes both.

Since most educators are not acquainted with the details contained in the appendix, they are not in a position to agree or disagree with all of them. We assure our readers, however, that we have given many years of thought to this elaboration of critical thinking, and that it has profited from intense scrutiny by many specialists. Our choices of emphasis and categorizations make good sense, even though we realize there are other possible reasonable ones.

There is, however, one significant controversy. The concern is whether critical thinking facility is subject-matter specific, a general facility applicable across different subjects, or a combination of both. If critical thinking facility is completely subject-matter specific, then there is an entirely or largely different set of critical thinking abilities and dispositions for each subject: mathematics, history, literature, and so on. If, at the other extreme, critical thinking is a general facility, then critical thinking abilities and dispositions are readily applicable and transferable to all subjects, including out-of-school "subjects," such as purchasing, testifying, and borrowing. Obviously, there are many possible positions between these two extremes.

We cannot argue this theoretical issue in this book. However, we do hold a position. We believe that critical thinking abilities and dispositions have both general and subject-specific features. They are applicable to different school subjects, and to a wide variety of activities requiring good thinking which do not fall under school subjects. At the same time, we believe that for children to learn how to employ critical thinking, they have to be instructed in the use of the abilities and dispositions in a wide variety of contexts. We also believe that actual critical thinking activity requires knowledge of the topic and the context. The examples in volume 1 of lessons designed by teachers for teaching critical thinking in specific subjects represent a recognition by practitioners of this point of view.

What are the implications of this position for the evaluation of critical thinking? If you wish to know whether students can think critically in science, literature, or history, the information gathering should be done within the context of problems in those subjects. If, on the other hand, you wish to evaluate students' critical thinking facility in general and thus estimate the likelihood that they will think critically in new contexts, students should be presented with a wide variety of critical thinking tasks requiring background knowledge they already possess. It is obvious that the number of possible tasks requiring critical thinking is very large, so not all types of tasks can be represented in any evaluation. However, attention to diversity is important. We will treat the comprehensiveness of critical thinking evaluation in more detail in chapter 2.

A further implication for evaluation is that our position enables us meaningfully to ask the question, "Under what conditions does critical thinking instruction in school subject matter transfer to everyday life outside of school?" If critical thinking is totally subject specific, then the answer is that critical thinking transfers only to the extent that school subject matter is applicable to the solution of everyday problems. In this extreme view, helping people to think critically in the unlimited number of areas that are not school subjects is an unattainable goal. There would be no point in having such a goal, or in evaluating the degree to which it has been reached.

>> *A defensible educational ideal*

The reasons supporting critical thinking, as we have defined it, as an educational ideal are based on a philosophy of education which maintains that education should transform people's character and way of living. Our ideal of the educated person includes being able to exercise autonomy in making important decisions; respecting the rights and autonomy of others; and seeking not only factual information but also an understanding of why things are as they are. The model of critical thinking offered can support this transformation. Thinking critically as we have defined it involves asking for reasons and being open-minded to others' points of view. In addition, since the process is directed toward decisions about belief and action, it supports an individual's autonomy.

Thinking critically as we have defined it also requires having a certain *attitude*. To be a critical thinker is to be a particular type of person:

- one who is open to the views of others;
- one who does not jump to conclusions, but bases action and belief on good reasons;
- one who wishes critical thinking to be directed equally to his or her own thinking.

These attitudes are essential for the autonomous person in a democratic society.

Critical thinking as presented in this chapter involves much more than appraisal, and differs greatly from criticism in the negative sense and "tearing things down." Thinking critically includes many creative activities, such as formulating hypotheses, conceiving of and stating definitions, planning courses of action to meet some goal, inferring, and gauging a given audience and presenting a position it can understand. This breadth in critical thinking provides a comprehensive concept of thinking for approaching decisions about belief or action.

>> *Usefulness of the definition for educational decisions*

The definition is useful for instruction, curriculum development, and evaluation. The usefulness stems primarily from the detailed lists of topics which are suggested in the tables. The lists of topics can provide content specifications for instructional planning and for developing tests or other types of techniques for gathering information on students' critical thinking. If, for instance, you wished to evaluate basic support-related abilities, topics 4 and 5 of the appendix outline targets for gathering information. In evaluating ability to judge the credibility of a source, for example, the table directs you to reflect on such matters as whether students consider the expertise and degree of conflict of interest of the source. Similar direction can be obtained from the other topics of the table.

>> *A role for judgment in critical thinking*

The definition provides both for the use of rules and for judgment in critical thinking. For example, the appendix lists Investigating as topic 7-c, which includes the topic, Designing Experiments. Experiments should be designed to control factors not under investigation so that they have no part in the outcome of the investigation. This is a rule of experimental design which we will discuss in chapter 6. However, application of that rule to a particular case always involves the use of judgment. This is so since no experiment can control all factors not under consideration; there are just too many of them. Thus, the experimenter has to use judgment based upon experience in the field to decide which factors to take into account and which to ignore.

Similar room for judgment can be found among the critical thinking dispositions. For example, the dispositions to try to be well informed and to seek as much precision as the subject permits require the use of judgment based on experience. There is no rule to tell a person how well informed to be and no rule saying how much precision a subject permits.

Evaluating Raywift's letter also requires good judgment. Raywift offered some good reasons for his position, but also some poor ones. How are these strengths and weaknesses to be weighed and balanced in reaching a final judgment about whether to agree with his proposed action? There are no rules or formulas for doing this weighing and balancing, but it must be done. Good judgment is what is needed.

The implications of this feature of our definition for evaluating critical thinking are profound. Evaluating critical thinking in all its aspects would require evaluating the use of good judgment as well as the use of critical thinking rules. It is difficult to evaluate such an elusive entity as good judgment, but some possible approaches are discussed in chapter 5.

Summary

This chapter has addressed the question, "What is critical thinking?" We have begun a book on evaluating critical thinking with this question because its answer is a prerequisite to beginning any evaluation.

The core of critical thinking, as we conceive it, is reasonable and reflective thinking that is focused upon deciding what to believe or do. This definition has been represented in pictorial form as a process of inference leading from some basic support to a decision about belief or action. The process takes place in a context of problem solving and interacting with the world and other people, and is permeated with attempts to maintain clarity and to exhibit critical thinking dispositions.

Each part of the pictorial has been detailed as a list of topics which might be evaluated. The topics cover sets of abilities and dispositions which go together to make up critical thinking. The abilities include clarity-related abilities, inference-related abilities, basic support-related abilities, and abilities to use strategies and tactics for going about the critical thinking process in an orderly and effective way. The dispositions rest fundamentally on open-mindedness and the desire to use one's critical thinking abilities on others' and one's own thinking.

Our precise, one-sentence definition of critical thinking is widely accepted among educators. Our detailed definition is defensible as an educational ideal; detailed enough to provide guidance for educational decisions; oriented to practical situations; and open enough to allow for the exercise of good judgment. We do not claim that it is the only reasonable definition possible. However, it is more complete than others that exist today.

Suggested Readings

Costa, A. (Ed.) (1985). *Developing Minds: A Resource Book for Teaching Thinking, Part III.* Association for Supervision and Curriculum Development, 225 N. Washington Street, Alexandria, VA 22314.

Ennis, R. (1981). Rational thinking and educational practice. In Soltis (Ed.), *Philosophy and Education, Vol. 1 of the Eightieth Yearbook of the National Society for the Study of Education.* Chicago: NSSE, 143-183.

——— (1987). A taxonomy of critical thinking dispositions and abilities. In Baron and Sternberg (Eds.), *Teaching Thinking Skills: Theory and Practice.* New York: W.H. Freeman, 9-26.

Norris, S. (1984). Defining observational competence. *Science Education, 68,* 129-142.

Walsh, D. and Paul, R. (1986). *The Goal of Critical Thinking: From Educational Ideal to Educational Reality, Chapter II.* American Federation of Teachers, 555 New Jersey Avenue, Washington, D.C.

CHAPTER TWO

GATHERING QUALITY INFORMATION ON STUDENTS' CRITICAL THINKING

Any evaluation involving critical thinking, whether it be of teachers, teaching techniques, programs, schools, or districts, depends upon information gathered on students' critical thinking. The first section of this chapter will deal with some of the different techniques which can be used to gather information on critical thinking and with the way the chosen technique can affect the quality of that information. The second section will discuss the breadth of coverage of attempts to gather information on critical thinking. The final section will discuss the two major indicators of the quality of information used in educational evaluation—*validity* and *reliability*. This final section is somewhat more theoretical than the others, and many of the ideas in it are difficult. If you work through it, however, your time will be well spent.

Section One: Types of Information-gathering Techniques

We have used the expression "information-gathering techniques" to refer to all the assorted techniques that might be used to collect information on students' critical thinking. In this first section we will examine some of the more widely used techniques, and speak to advantages and disadvantages of each, referring specifically to considerations of their reliability and validity.

Before we begin, we wish to give brief definitions of reliability and validity. The reliability of a test is the consistency of student performance, using the same individuals, from one administration of the test to another. The validity of a test is the degree to which scores on the test can be trusted to mean what they are purported to mean. (If, before going on, you want more information than this about these two terms, you should read section three of this chapter.)

This section is meant to provide a general overview of the advantages and disadvantages of various possible types of information-gathering techniques. More detailed information on specific techniques is contained in later chapters: chapter 3 discusses commercially available critical thinking tests; chapter 4 discusses the construction of multiple-choice tests; and chapter 5 describes how open-ended approaches might be designed.

>> *Multiple-choice tests*

The use of multiple-choice tests is a very common way to gather information on students' critical thinking. The general format of the technique is known to all educators: there is either a set of questions with a choice of several answers for each, or a set of specific lead-in phrases with a choice of several ways to complete each phrase. Usually, there is a single correct or best answer for each item, and students are usually graded on the number of items they answer correctly.

One of the major advantages of the multiple-choice format is the ease and speed of acquiring reproducible scoring results. That is, with minimal training almost any person can quickly score the tests and arrive at the same grade as anyone else. It is also possible to use machines to score answer sheets, increasing even more the speed and reproducibility of scoring.

Another advantage of the multiple-choice format is that many specific probes can be made of students' critical thinking abilities and dispositions. That is, since each item usually takes students only a short time to answer, they have the time to answer many items on different aspects of critical thinking. This fact seems to lead to the further advantage of providing a quick diagnosis of students' critical thinking deficiencies.

A further advantage of multiple-choice tests is that generally they can be constructed to provide reasonably consistent results.

Also, since reliability generally can be increased by providing more items on a test, the reliability of a multiple-choice critical thinking test can be readily increased by adding more items.

However, it is some of the alleged strengths of multiple-choice testing that lead many people to criticize it as a technique for gathering information about students' critical thinking. The fact that items generally have one correct or best response, for example, makes many persons suspect the suitability of the technique. This suspicion is based on the fact that issues requiring critical thinking often do not have a single correct or best answer. Thus, one possible, yet undesirable, implication of the use of multiple-choice tests is that students would come to believe that critical thinking always leads or should lead to one correct or best answer.

Others criticize multiple-choice tests for not providing any indication of the thinking processes which students use to arrive at their answers. Answer sheets give no indication of whether students thought their way to the answers in reasonable or unreasonable ways. In other words, the inference from how students perform (the answers they mark on their answer sheets), to how they were thinking, and thence to the abilities they have, is quite a large one.

Our perspective is that multiple-choice tests do have a role in collecting information on students' critical thinking. For example, if there are a large number of principles which we would like students to know, such as those associated with judging the credibility of sources, then multiple-choice tests using credibility items of the sort advocated in chapter 4 are useful. Also, if information is desired on how well, in general, a group of students can use certain critical thinking abilities, then multiple-choice tests are valuable. This perspective is, however, predicated on the belief that the validity of multiple-choice critical thinking tests can be improved. It may be possible to achieve this through greater concentration during the design of such tests on the thinking processes of students as they answer items. This topic will be discussed under "Drafting Items" in chapter 4.

Multiple-choice tests are not adequate, however, as the only technique for gathering information on students' critical thinking. While they might provide good information on separate abilities, they are not suited to providing information on the ability of students to employ several abilities together while working on a complex problem. In addition, multiple-choice tests are not useful for providing information on students' dispositions to think critically. In general, dispositions need to be examined in situations where students have considerable control over the course of their thinking and where, if they display particular abilities, they have done so spontaneously. So, for instance, if we wish to gather information on whether students have the disposition to consider alternatives, we need to place them in a situation where not only considering alternatives is valued, but also where the students themselves must realize this. We find it difficult to imagine how a multiple-choice test can satisfy these requirements.

>> *Constructed-response tests*

Constructed-response tests of critical thinking come in several forms. A useful distinction is between those that require several short, written pieces in response to relatively specific questions or directives, and those that require more extended essays in response to relatively general questions or directives. In addition, while we use the term "tests," we mean to include essays such as term papers.

In general, the advantages of constructed-response tests offset the disadvantages of multiple-choice tests and vice versa. Two of the major disadvantages involve scoring and reliability. Constructed-response tests are far more difficult and time-consuming to score than multiple-choice tests. The need for extra time is obvious. The difficulty of scoring arises because the scorer must have training in critical thinking and usually must be able to make wise decisions about those student responses that do not fit the typical mold. Guidelines for scoring can be provided, but because of the nature of constructed-responses, no set of guidelines can cover all possibilities.

Constructed-response tests are generally less consistently scored than multiple-choice tests. This stems from the difficulty in specifying completely how constructed responses are to be graded. For example, different raters grading the same essay or the same rater grading the same essay on different occasions often produce different scores. In addition, it is difficult to estimate the consistency of subjects' responses from one occasion to another except by having them write the test more than once. But this leads to problems due to interactions between each trial as discussed later under "Reliability."

The disadvantages of constructed-response tests are offset by a number of advantages. First, they allow examinees more leeway in answering and also usually allow for more than one legitimate approach to a problem. This feature helps avoid the criticism of multiple-choice tests that the requirement of one correct or best answer is artificial.

Second, constructed-response tests of the essay sort provide a means for seeing whether students can coordinate a number of critical thinking abilities in working on a complex problem. Are students, for instance, able to judge the credibility of the information they have at their disposal and use the credible information to make sound inferences to a decision? Are they able to analyze someone else's decision process and ask questions about various aspects of the process?

Third, constructed-response tests, especially essays tests, provide a means of gathering information on students' critical thinking dispositions. If students are given a general task, such as evaluating a position taken by someone, then their essays can show whether they sought reasons for the person's position, whether they looked for alternatives to what the person said, and whether they were open-minded about the person's position. If students did these things without being specifically instructed to do so, then this is evidence that they have the related critical thinking dispositions.

Fourth, constructed-response tests often provide more clearly valid information on students' critical thinking abilities and dispositions than multiple-choice tests. For example, suppose we wish to gather information on students' ability to judge the credibility of sources. In a multiple-choice format, examinees might be presented with two sources of information and asked to choose the more believable. But as we shall show in chapter 4, we cannot be sure, without further information, whether or not students who choose the right answer do so because they know how to judge correctly the credibility of sources. On a constructed-response test, in addition to indicating which source is more believable, examinees might be asked to provide reasons for their judgements. With this additional information, we can make more trustworthy inferences about students' ability to judge correctly the credibility of sources.

>> *Direct classroom observation*

Direct classroom observation typically attempts to record some aspects of an ongoing classroom situation while disturbing the normal course of events in that classroom to the smallest degree possible. A usual criterion of successful direct observation is *ecological validity*. An observation is ecologically valid if it represents what happens in normal situations, in the ecology of ordinary life situations. Ecological validity is achieved through the observer's trying to control to the least extent possible what occurs in the classroom and being satisfied to accept what happens. The observer thus tries, so to speak, to be a fly on the wall.

An important advantage of such an approach is that it gives an indication of normal critical thinking performance. Normal performance in this sense is contrasted to optimal performance, which might be gauged using a more formalized information-gathering technique. Optimal performance refers to the critical thinking performance that can be expected from an individual or group of individuals under the best of conditions. Normal critical thinking performance is the level at which people think critically in the course of their everyday affairs. Thus, comparing the results of direct classroom observation of students' critical thinking with their thinking on standardized tests, which they are often motivated to pass for specific rewards, can give an indication of the disposition of the students to think critically in their everyday lives.

Direct classroom observation can take several forms. First, it can be more or less open-ended in that the observer simply "views the students' critical thinking," without looking for anything in particular. On the other hand, the observation can be circumscribed by focusing on particular aspects of critical thinking. For example, the observer may watch for the occurrence of ten different practices, including students seeking reasons, withholding judgment, applying criteria to evaluate the credibility of information, and making distinctions between dictionary meanings and stipulated meanings of words. The observer may simply record how many instances of each practice occur, or record also the number of students contributing to the occurrences.

In addition, direct observation of either the more general or more specific type can focus on a whole classroom of students at one time or on students one at a time. It is obvious that if students are to be observed one at a time, many problems exist. In order to be confident that the observations of any particular student are indicative of how that student generally behaves, it is necessary to observe that student on several occasions. Such an approach is so demanding on resources as to be justified only in very special circumstances, such as when detailed information on an individual is crucial for making some important decision about that person.

Observation of whole classes as units is also demanding on resources. In order to be confident of having an adequate indication of, for example, the critical thinking dispositions of a class of students, we need to make observations of the whole class on several occasions. To ensure greater representativeness, it is also preferable if these different observations occur in different circumstances. Thus, it is advisable to observe students being taught different subjects by different teachers.

Any observation technique also requires observers with high levels of expertise and understanding of critical thinking. This means that observers need to have thought deeply about critical thinking and its manifestations before starting to observe.

>> *Individual interviews*

Individual interviewing is another technique for gathering information on students' critical thinking that makes heavy demands on resources but that can serve very useful purposes. This technique, when used properly, is usually better than any other for acquiring information on the thinking processes that students follow when working on problems. Thus, there is the possibility of making more trustworthy inferences from students' performance to their critical thinking abilities and dispositions.

One prime source of invalidity, however, arises from the nature of the interaction between the interviewer and the student. In typical situations, the student is asked to work on a task in the presence of the interviewer. In general, the best approach is to initiate the interview with fairly open-ended instructions that do not severely restrict the sort of response the student can give. For example, the initial instruction might be for the student to work on the problem and to try to say everything that comes to his or her mind while doing so.

If the student is clearly thinking about the problem but not talking, then the interviewer can probe with nondirective questions like, "What are you thinking now?" or "Can you tell me what you are thinking now?" When it is clear that the student has said all he or she is going to say with such indirect probing, the interviewer might contemplate using more specific probes. For example, the interviewer might ask the student to justify a particular step in his or her solution: "Can you tell me why you did that?" In addition, the interviewer might be interested in whether specific considerations were part of the student's thinking: "When you were working on the problem, did it make any difference that the experiment was done only once?" or "Did the timing of the experiment affect your thinking in any way?"

It must be realized that directive probes may put thoughts into students' heads that would not otherwise have been there. Depending upon the context, this effect may or may not be desirable. For example, if the aim is to identify a particular student's thinking problems and to identify ways to help solve those problems, then directive probes can be useful. Suppose, for instance, a student is having difficulty with a problem but, when asked whether a certain fact from his or her background knowledge makes any difference to thinking about the problem, the student immediately sees how the problem is to be solved. Then, this interaction indicates that the student was not paying sufficient attention to background knowledge and that instruction which focused on doing this may have been helpful.

>> *Student and teacher journals*

Student and teacher journals contain records of and reflections on what has occurred in school. Under certain circumstances, journals can be useful sources of information in evaluating students' critical thinking. As with any information-gathering technique, it has limitations. For example, student journals are often intended to be largely undirected records or reflections. Since there is little control over what appears in journals of this type, teachers might not receive information on aspects of students' thinking that have particular interest.

However, journals can be directed if the teacher asks students to reflect or report on particular sorts of things. For example, high school social studies students might be asked to keep a journal in which they reflect on the major news items of each day. A class of elementary school students might be asked to keep a journal for science class in which they report upon the activities of each day's science class and suggest how they might have conducted the activities in a better way. Journals of this sort can be useful for examining trends in the growth of students' critical thinking dispositions. Teachers can read the journals and comment on them as they see fit, looking for indications of open-mindedness, seeking reasons, trying to be well informed, taking into account the total situation, and so on. For example, a student would indicate a disposition to be well informed or would show growth in this disposition if he or she began to look to more than one information source for news on the leading stories of the day. An elementary science student would show the same disposition by exploring the topic of the day's science activity in the encyclopedia at home.

As we indicated in chapter 1, critical thinking dispositions are essential to critical thinking. Given their importance and the difficulty of evaluating dispositions in traditional paper and pencil tests, teachers need to look for alternative approaches to evaluating them. Regularly kept student journals are one such source of information. Another source is the teacher's own journal. At the end of each class or day, teachers can make journal entries which report and reflect on information relevant to the evaluation of students' critical thinking. For example, records of concrete examples of evidence for or against critical thinking dispositions can be used to help assess students' growth in this area.

Suppose that the teacher concludes from records made at the beginning of the year that when students discuss some issue on which there is, for example, a divergence of opinion, they show little tolerance for views opposing their own. Suppose, by the middle of the semester, the teacher concludes from the journal that students are more willing to listen to alternative points of view. Then, if the teacher's conclusions are correct, this indicates that students have become more open-minded.

Just as with other information gathering techniques, journal information can be evaluated on the standards of reliability and validity. In general, journal keeping and interpretation lie more towards the art than the science end of the evaluation spectrum. That is, it is very difficult to assign any numbers indicating their reliability and validity. Because there are no standardized procedures for collecting journal information, we can expect that it is not very reliable. If it were possible to relive the whole series of situations, it is doubtful that exactly the same information would appear in the journals.

If, however, the meaning we attach to information in journals and the conclusions drawn from that information is that it reflects the impressions of "the experienced eye," then journals can be quite valid. Many educators believe that not all educational qualities can be reduced to numbers, because they believe that so much of education remains an art. If this is so, then the informed judgment of the trained practitioner based upon records kept over a period of time certainly can lead to valid educational conclusions.

>> *Section summary*

We have examined several types of techniques for gathering information on students' critical thinking: multiple-choice and constructed-response tests, direct classroom observation, individual interviewing, and student and teacher journals. Each technique can serve some purposes better than other techniques and no technique can serve all purposes we might have in evaluating students' critical thinking. Evaluators must take into account the purpose for which the information gathering will be done and choose a technique or techniques consonant with that purpose.

Section Two: Comprehensiveness of Critical Thinking Coverage

Gathering information about students' critical thinking can vary in comprehensiveness and in means of approach. Information-gathering techniques can cover different aspects of critical thinking, can be based on different types of knowledge, and can require students to work on different types of tasks. This section will outline some of these possibilities and discuss choosing among them. In chapter 3 we discuss in more detail the relative comprehensiveness of critical thinking coverage found among commercially available tests. The discussions in this section will help in recognizing their strengths and limitations.

>> *Aspect-specific techniques*

An *aspect-specific information-gathering technique* for evaluating students' critical thinking focuses on a single aspect of critical thinking, such as ability to identify assumptions, ability to judge the credibility of sources, inductive reasoning ability, or ability in defining. Such approaches are useful when we need detailed information on specific aspects of critical thinking. For example, even the ability to judge the credibility of sources is quite complex, since it involves the use of several criteria (as outlined in the appendix, topics 4 and 5). Therefore, in order to obtain a good picture of which criteria students know and which they do not know, and to obtain some indication of whether students can use the criteria in a variety of situations, evaluators need to present a large number of tasks. An approach concentrated in this way would be able to provide more detailed diagnostic information on particular aspects of critical thinking than an approach which covered a greater number of aspects.

>> *Comprehensive techniques*

An information-gathering technique that includes some tasks on each of the five broad areas of critical thinking (clarity-related abilities, inference-related abilities, basic support-related abilities, strategies and tactics, and dispositions) would be called a *comprehensive information-gathering technique*. However, as you will see in chapter 3, not all critical thinking tests fall neatly into either the aspect-specific or comprehensive category. Some tests may cover three or four of the five broad areas. We often conclude in such cases that they cover enough to be called comprehensive. Some tests may cover two broad areas. Such tests fall between the aspect-specific and comprehensive .

All other things being equal, comprehensive techniques clearly cannot provide as high quality diagnostic information on particular aspects of critical thinking as aspect-specific techniques. For example, a comprehensive technique might be able to gather information on students' knowledge of only three or four criteria for judging the credibility of sources. Therefore, given this sort of unrepresentative coverage, it is generally not justifiable to draw conclusions about specific aspects of critical thinking from comprehensive information-gathering techniques.

>> *General-knowledge techniques*

A *general-knowledge information-gathering technique* for evaluating critical thinking does not call for special knowledge of any particular discipline or school subject. Asking students to compare critically the coverage of a news event by various media, to devise a plan for obtaining a better turnout at student council elections, or to appraise critically a letter to the editor of a newspaper, do not directly call upon special knowledge from particular school subjects. Of course, it may be that in any such general-knowledge task, some special knowledge of such subjects as history, science, or literature is useful.

Techniques which rely on general knowledge can serve well some purposes in evaluating students' critical thinking. First, since advanced knowledge from particular school subjects is not needed, but knowledge from many areas can be brought to bear on the tasks, students are not penalized when they do not have particular pieces of advanced knowledge from school subjects.

There is a second reason for using general-knowledge information-gathering techniques. Many educators intend that critical thinking be applicable to people's everyday lives, where general knowledge is often more useful than special knowledge of school subjects. If general application is one of the goals of critical thinking instruction, then it would make sense to devise evaluations in line with that goal. Then we can check for a transfer of critical thinking abilities and dispositions from school contexts to everyday concerns.

>> *Subject-specific techniques*

Subject-specific information-gathering techniques test for critical thinking in specific school subjects. Thus, there can be critical thinking tests in science, history, art, and so on. Each would reflect the aspects of critical thinking which have been emphasized in that subject and would use special knowledge from that subject. Such subject-specific techniques differ from general-knowledge techniques in an important way. If an evaluation technique purports to be gathering information on students' critical thinking while relying only on general knowledge, then it is legitimate to complain if advanced knowledge of particular scientific, historical, or artistic facts is required. However, if a technique is specific to science, history, or art, and the facts required are ones that have been taught, this complaint cannot be legitimately raised.

The use of subject-specific and general-knowledge evaluation techniques, like anything else in critical thinking evaluation, requires some caution. In particular, it is risky to generalize from performance on one type of technique to performance on another. By this we mean that if, for instance, you have gathered some information on students' critical thinking in history, then this is not sufficient evidence for saying how well they would think critically in science, in literature, or in tasks requiring general knowledge. It would be desirable to be able to make such generalizations safely. However, until more is known about how people learn and transfer critical thinking, prudence suggests gathering information in a variety of contexts if conclusions about critical thinking in a variety of contexts are desired.

The distinction between subject-specific and general-knowledge techniques is not a sharp one and depends to some extent on the level of the student tested. But the distinction is still a useful one in discussions of critical thinking testing, as the previous paragraphs show.

>> *Techniques with a variety of tasks*

Multiple-choice tests, constructed-response tests, individual interviews, and other information-gathering techniques each present students with different tasks. The use of different sorts of tasks is usually desirable.

Performing well on evaluations of critical thinking is not an end in itself. We wish to teach students critical thinking so that they will be better persons and so that they will live more fruitful and happier lives. This will require

- thinking critically in academic situations as well as in everyday situations;

- thinking critically when one is writing as well as when one is speaking;

- thinking critically when the task is relatively circumscribed as well as when the task in relatively open-ended; and

- thinking critically when alone and when dealing with other people in group situations.

Evaluations of critical thinking are usually artificial in comparison to the life situations in which we hope students will eventually be able and disposed to think critically. Therefore, we must keep in mind that we are trying to generalize from some more-or-less artificial evaluation situation to some more-or-less real-life situation. Such generalizations always contain some error. One way to reduce the error is to use a variety of tasks in evaluating students' critical thinking.

If students do well on an evaluation and the only type of information-gathering techniques that were used were pencil-and-paper multiple-choice tests, it is risky to conclude that students will be able to think well beyond such tasks. If, on the other hand, the information gathering techniques included multiple-choice tests, constructed-response tests, direct classroom observation, and individual interviewing, then conclusions about how well students will think critically outside the evaluation situation can be more trustworthy. If, as well, the evaluation spans a variety of situations, such as those in the bulleted list on the previous page, then inferences about students' critical thinking can be even more trustworthy.

Section Three: Indicators of Quality

In chapter 1 critical thinking was defined as a process of reasonable and reflective thinking. The logic of the process involves providing a sound basis for thinking and making legitimate inferences from that basis to some decision about what to believe or do (although as we said in chapter 1 the direction of the process is not fixed). This emphasis on the *process* of thinking over its *products* is based on the fact that many conclusions of human thought, even the most profound ones, may someday be shown to be at least partly in error. In other words, people may have reasoned well, even though the conclusions of their reasoning are wrong. In addition, we emphasize the process of thinking because merely having information is not enough; we also need to know how to use the information to make decisions and to solve problems.

The process orientation of critical thinking has an important consequence for judging the quality of information about people's thinking. The consequence is that we cannot judge the quality of information on people's thinking solely on the basis of what the information tells us about their beliefs and actions. Rather, we must judge the quality of the information on the basis of what it tells us about the thinking processes which led to those beliefs and actions. More specifically, we can say that the information gathered on students' critical thinking is of high quality when it allows us to decide whether or not the students' thinking processes were justified.

In the educational evaluation field there have traditionally been two indicators of the quality of information: *reliability* and *validity.* Both are technical terms in testing, but reliability is given a technical meaning which is somewhat different from its everyday usage. We have used reliability in its technical sense so far in this chapter, but since there is this risk of confusing this technical meaning with the everyday meaning of reliability, care must be exercised when using the concept .

Recall that at the beginning of the chapter we warned that this section is more theoretical and somewhat more difficult than the previous ones. However, these ideas are very important for understanding how tests are judged to be good or bad.

>> *Reliability*

Everyday and technical senses of reliability compared. In everyday discourse, when we say that something is reliable we mean that we can depend upon it or trust it to do what it is supposed to do. We say that a hot water heater is reliable because we can trust it, day-after-day, to provide the amount of hot water it is supposed to give. A taxi service is reliable when it can be trusted to pick us up on time and to efficiently and safely deliver us to our destination. A weather forecasting service is reliable when the information provided is up-to-date and accurate.

The above uses of the word "reliable" are different from the technical use in educational evaluation. The technical use is narrower: an information-gathering technique is reliable if it yields *consistent* results from one occasion to another. According to this definition, to say that the hot water heater is reliable is to say only that its results are consistent. If that result were stone-cold water when the setting was on hot, it would not matter. As long as the output was consistent, it would still be reliable, according to the technical definition of reliability. The taxi service would be reliable if its taxis were consistently late or they consistently got lost on the way to our destination. The weather service would be considered reliable according to the technical notion if it consistently forecast hotter temperatures than were forthcoming. Similarly, a technique for gathering information on critical thinking would be reliable as long as it yielded the same results when given more than once to the same individuals. In a parallel manner, a technique for gathering information on critical thinking could be reliable in the technical sense and not be gathering information on critical thinking at all!

The technical notion of reliability differs significantly from the one in everyday use. If you read a manual for a critical thinking test that reports the test to be reliable, and you interpret this to mean that the test is a trustworthy indicator of critical thinking, then you have read more into the technical concept than was intended. If for "reliability in the technical sense" you read "consistency," you will not be far from the intended meaning.

The importance of having technical reliability. Consistency of information is one very important indicator of quality. If, for example, every time in the space of a few minutes the gas gauge of your car showed a different reading, this would indicate a problem with the gauge. For the gauge to be trustworthy it is *necessary* that it be consistent. However, being consistent is not *sufficient* for it to be trustworthy. For example, the gauge can consistently give too high or too low a reading. If the amount that it is too high or too low is consistent, then we probably can compensate. We learn that when the gauge is on one-fourth, it is time to get gas. On the other hand, because of some malfunction the gauge might consistently provide readings of the voltage generated by the car's alternator. In such a case, while perfectly consistent, the gauge is absolutely untrustworthy as an indicator of how much gas is in the tank.

Similar remarks can be made about information gathered on critical thinking. Consistency is necessary but not sufficient for the information to be trustworthy. The information can be absolutely consistent, but analogously to the gas gauge indicating alternator voltage, it can be indicating nothing about levels of critical thinking. For example, imagine a test purported to test for critical thinking in science. However, answering correctly the items on the test requires only rote memorization: one item might ask the question, "What is the formula for water?" and accept as correct the answer "H_2O." Such a test might be highly reliable in the technical sense, but would indicate nothing about levels of critical thinking, despite its advertised purpose.

Obtaining estimates of reliability. One further caution about the technical notion of reliability is in order. The reliability of a technique could be determined by using it to collect information from the same individuals on at least two separate occasions and then comparing the results. To the degree that the results are the same on both occasions, then the technique would be considered reliable. Such an approach faces several problems, however, which can be illustrated by the following example.

Imagine a test designed to collect information on students' ability to identify when people unfairly change the meaning of crucial terms in the middle of discussions. The test contains a number of letters to an editor, let us suppose, and a scale for rating students' responses. A group of students is given the test and answers are rated. In order to see how reliable the test is, it is administered to the students again the following day. Their responses are again rated and the results from the two administrations correlated. In all likelihood the correlation is less than perfect. Why? Our knowledge of human beings would suggest that some students learned several things on the first trial that they were able to apply to the second trial. Some students might have discussed the test with other people and applied things learned from these discussions to the second trial. Perhaps some students were more tired during one trial than the other. Thus, there are several reasons why students might have performed differently on the second trial, making the second set of results somewhat inconsistent with the first. In this way, human beings are not like most inanimate objects. If a gas gauge is giving erratic results, then we suspect the instrument. We do not expect the gas level to be affected by our attempts to determine the amount of gas. However, we can expect people to be affected by trying to find out how well they think critically.

Split-half reliability. Because attempts to study characteristics of human beings can change the very characteristics being studied, evaluators have devised approaches for estimating the reliability of an information-gathering instrument from just one administration. The approach works for techniques that can be divided into units. Examples would include a test with a number of items or an interview schedule with a number of questions; that is, techniques that yield some summary score, such as the total number of items or questions answered correctly.

Let us suppose, for purposes of example, that we are dealing with a fifty-item test. To estimate the reliability of the test, it would be given to a sample of examinees. Then, in the simplest approach, the test items would be divided in half in some way, such as by placing the first twenty-five items in one half and the second twenty-five in the other; by placing the even-numbered items in one half and the odd-numbered ones in the other; or by dividing each part of the test into halves and combining all the first halves and all the second halves. The reliability would then be estimated by correlating examinees' total scores on the resulting halves. This approach and its variations constitute the *split-half* method of estimating reliability.

Kuder-Richardson reliability. The effect of calculating a Kuder-Richardson reliability is as follows: first, the items on a test are divided in half in all possible ways; second, the split-half reliability is calculated for each pair of halves; and third, the average of these split-half reliabilities is calculated. (In practice, the mathematical formula used does not reveal all of these steps.) Kuder-Richardson reliability estimates are high to the extent that scores on individual items on the test correlate with one another, and low to the extent that they do not correlate. This sort of estimate may be quite inappropriate for tests of various aspects of critical thinking because there is no theoretical reason for believing that all the items on such tests should correlate highly with one another. Thus, it might be the case that some types of critical thinking tests should be judged better if their reliabilities estimated in this way were low! This surprising fact points to a problem in using reliability estimated by standard evaluation methods for judging the quality of critical thinking tests.

Critical thinking tests generally have lower estimated reliabilities than other standardized tests, such as, for example, intelligence tests. Reliability estimates tend to range from about .65 to .75, and tend to increase with the level of sophistication of examinees. We recommend that reliabilities within this range should be considered adequate and that very high reliabilities, especially on tests purporting to test a variety of aspects of critical thinking, should not be considered automatically better than more moderate ones.

Interrater reliability. Some types of information-gathering techniques do not divide sensibly into units, or the total number of units is so small that, when divided, there are very few in each half. An example of a technique that cannot be sensibly divided into units is one that calls for a single essay response. A technique with too few units to divide in half and have anything like equivalent halves might be a test requiring six short-answer responses, each examining a different aspect of critical thinking. Either situation makes it inappropriate to use the techniques discussed above for estimating reliability. One solution is to resort to using the information-gathering technique on more than one occasion with the same examinees. The problems of prior administrations affecting later ones are, of course, present in such an approach. However, the inaccuracies resulting from these problems might be offset by having at least some estimate of the reliability of the technique.

Another approach is to rely on interrater reliability. Techniques which do not divide easily into units often need to be graded by an expert rater. For example, an essay cannot be graded by machine as can a multiple-choice test . Someone who has been trained and has expertise in grading the essay must do the job. A concern is that different expert raters might give vastly different ratings. To check this, different raters, each trained in the task, can grade examinees' responses to the technique and their ratings correlated to provide an indication of interrater reliability. Interrater reliability thus gives an estimate of the consistency of grades across different graders. But the original concern of technical-reliability estimation is with the consistency of subjects' responses from occasion to occasion. So, interrater reliability cannot replace estimates of reliability in its original technical sense.

Summary remarks about reliability. In this section we have cautioned against an uncritical interpretation of the reported reliabilities of techniques for gathering information on critical thinking. Our aim is to make you an informed and wary consumer of critical thinking evaluation devices. Nevertheless, we stress that reliability as consistency of collected information from one occasion to another is a desirable goal in gathering information on students' critical thinking. Information should be collected to promote the highest consistency desirable.

Many factors are known to affect consistency. Evaluators should ensure that, to the extent possible, these factors are controlled. It is known that personal factors (e.g., level of fatigue, degree of motivation, understanding of the task) and environmental factors (e.g., levels of comfort, lighting, and noise) can all affect consistency. Common sense can help to ensure that such factors do not substantially affect test scores. In addition, taking care to provide unambiguous instructions and questions also increases consistency.

Reliabilities appear in test manuals as stark, apparently unambiguous numbers, quite different from the picture we have painted in this section. We have said that it is difficult to know what level of reported reliability is desirable in a technique for gathering information on critical thinking. To say otherwise would, in our view, be misleading. People gathering information on critical thinking must realize the primitive state of the art. Good sense is demanded in judging the level of reliability needed for the use to which the information will be put. Clearly, the more individual-specific and important the use for the information, the greater the reliability needed. However, it was mentioned previously that reliability in the sense of consistency is not enough. Information on students' critical thinking can be consistent, and consistently wrong. A standard of quality other than consistency is therefore required—the standard of validity.

>> *Validity*

Validity in educational evaluation is very similar to the everyday notion of reliability: *trustworthiness*. A procedure for evaluating students' critical thinking ability is valid if it can be *trusted* to tell us the extent to which the students have critical thinking ability. More precisely, an evaluation procedure is valid in a particular situation to the extent that it measures what it is supposed to measure in that situation. (This approach to validity is not the only one. However, for reasons beyond the scope of this book, it seems to us to be better than the others.)

The reason for the qualification, "in a particular situation," is that a test might be a valid measure of critical thinking in one situation but not in another. Suppose, for example, that a test of algebra word problems written in English is taken by students whose first language is Spanish and who have difficulty with English. This test would be less valid for those students than for students whose first language is English. So without some reference to the situation, a statement about test validity is incomplete. No test is valid for all situations in which it might possibly be used.

There are three standard types of evidence for the validity of an evaluation device: criterion-related evidence, content-related evidence, and construct-related evidence. Since construct-related evidence includes the other two, this standard system of classification is not elegant, but it is serviceable.

Criterion-related evidence consists of correlations between test scores and some outside criterion, or indicator, for the same thing. For example, criterion-related evidence for the validity of an educational aptitude test might be obtained by correlating scores on the test with the degree of educational success later on, perhaps as indicated by grades. Unfortunately, there is no good outside criterion for critical thinking, so criterion-related evidence seems unavailable for critical thinking tests.

Content-related evidence is based upon analyses of the content that is supposed to be covered by the evaluation procedure and upon judgments that particular items or activities are actually good indicators of success in the content. This approach to validity leans very heavily on expert judgment and is common for critical thinking tests. In our later discussion of existing critical thinking tests, we shall make heavy use of this type of evidence about validity.

Construct-related evidence includes whatever is relevant to judgments about the extent to which a procedure tests for the construct it is supposed to test for in a particular situation. The word "construct" refers to underlying abilities, dispositions, or traits of human beings, as opposed to directly observable characteristics. Critical thinking is such a construct, as are anxiety, intelligence, aggressiveness, and open-mindedness. To have construct-related evidence for a test is to have evidence that it measures a particular construct. Such evidence can include criterion-related evidence, content-related evidence, correlations that are in accord with expectations (for example, a correlation between age and critical thinking test scores would be expected for students in the K-12 range), and results of teaching and experiments that are in accord with expectations. As an example of the latter type of evidence, we would expect students who are given high-quality instruction in critical thinking to improve their scores on a critical thinking test more than students who are not given any critical thinking instruction.

It is usually difficult to determine the construct validity of an approach for gathering information on critical thinking abilities or dispositions. This is because we can gather little, if any, *direct* evidence on underlying thinking abilities and dispositions. Consider any typical multiple-choice critical thinking test. All that is available on the answer sheets of such tests are the conclusions of students' thinking, not the processes that led them to those conclusions. However, it is the thinking process that is of prime importance because we know that students sometimes arrive at correct answers through poor thinking processes, and at incorrect answers through good thinking processes. Thus, we must make an inference from the conclusions of students' thinking to the construct, critical thinking, which we are trying to measure.

Even essay tests of critical thinking or in-depth interviews do not provide completely clear information on all that students think as they give their answers. It is true that essay tests and interviews provide more direct information on thinking processes than multiple-choice tests. Nevertheless, an inference has to be made from the essays students write and from what they say in interviews to the abilities and dispositions that they have.

In the case of evaluating critical thinking dispositions, the problem is compounded by an extra inferential step. To say that people are disposed to do something is to say that they will do that thing when appropriate. This presupposes that they are *able* to do whatever it is. Suppose we consider a task in which students are asked to interpret a poem. From what students say or write, we wish to decide whether or not they are disposed to consider alternatives. If they do consider *on the test* alternative interpretations of the poem, we still need to infer that they are disposed to do so in other situations. If they do not consider alternatives, it might be because they are unable or unaware of the need to do so, or they might be intimidated by the situation but disposed to consider alternatives in nontesting situations. Thus, if students do not consider alternative interpretations of the poem, is it because they are not disposed to consider alternatives (even though they are able to) or are they unable? The evaluator must make a series of inferences.

The point is that when we collect information on students' critical thinking, our concern is only secondarily with their performance. Our prime concern is with the abilities and dispositions that lie behind that performance and about which we must make inferences. The performance is only an indicator of what is our prime concern. The task of judging the validity of an information-gathering technique is a task of judging its trustworthiness as an indicator of underlying abilities and dispositions. Inference is required to move from the evidence of performance to statements about abilities and dispositions.

Chapter Summary

Quality information on students' critical thinking can be gathered using a variety of techniques that include multiple-choice tests, constructed-response tests, direct classroom observation, individual interviewing of students, and student and teacher journals. Each technique has advantages and disadvantages.

The breadth of coverage of information-gathering techniques can vary. Information can be gathered on a single aspect of critical thinking or on several aspects, and the information can rely on general knowledge or on the special knowledge of a particular subject. The uses of each of these approaches was discussed.

Any evaluation of students' critical thinking requires high-quality information about their thinking. Two indicators of quality were discussed, reliability and validity. In the field of educational evaluation, reliability is only consistency of information from one information-gathering occasion to another. In evaluation, reliability does not mean trustworthiness, as it does in everyday usage. In the evaluation field, the trustworthiness of information is called its validity. More precisely, a test is valid in a situation to the extent that it measures what it is supposed to measure in that situation. The phrase "in a situation" is important because, for example, a test might be a valid measure of critical thinking for some students but not for others. Categories of evidence for validity are criterion-related, content-related, and construct-related validity.

Finally, we refer you to chapters 3, 4, and 5, where the discussions of this chapter are extended and applied.

Suggested Readings

Norris, S. (1986). Evaluating critical thinking ability. *The History and Social Science Teacher, 21* (3), 135-146.

———— (1988). Controlling for background beliefs when developing multiple-choice critical thinking tests. *Educational Measurement, 7* (3), 5-11.

Standards for Educational and Psychological Testing. (1985). American Psychological Association, 1200 Seventeenth Street, NW, Washington, DC 20036.

CHAPTER THREE

COMMERCIALLY AVAILABLE CRITICAL THINKING TESTS

If you are starting this book here, you will find some terms which were explained earlier. Please check the glossary or index if you need help.

Although techniques for gathering information on students' critical thinking can, theoretically, come in a variety of forms, the only forms that are commercially available are tests. These are mostly multiple-choice and are based on general knowledge. Of the general knowledge critical thinking tests, all are multiple-choice except for one essay test. Some tests are comprehensive to a degree; others are aspect-specific. There are more comprehensive critical thinking tests than aspect-specific tests, which are available only for observation appraisal and deductive reasoning.

So far as we know, there are no commercially available, subject-specific critical thinking tests. Test of Enquiry Skills, a multiple-choice test that we shall describe, comes close to being a subject-specific critical thinking test. (Its third section is a test of critical thinking in science, and its first two sections test for critical thinking in both social studies and science.) A number of commercially available tests for school subjects do include critical thinking items, but we shall not attempt to describe these. They are too numerous and varied. We hope that our examination of general knowledge critical thinking tests will help you to examine subject-specific ones.

Given our discussion of the relationship between critical and creative thinking in chapter 1, we should mention that some tests of creative thinking probably test as well for aspects of critical thinking. However, we have chosen to examine only those tests which purport to be tests of critical thinking.

This chapter has two major sections. In the first section we review eight comprehensive critical thinking tests and in the second section, four aspect-specific tests. In both sections we use the tests to highlight a number of problems endemic to critical thinking testing.

Please realize that we are the authors of some of the tests reviewed, so we have a conflict of interest. We have tried to be unbiased in our reviews by indicating that the general problems of critical thinking testing are not solved by our instruments. We are also scholars working on solving the problems of testing for critical thinking. So when we see some partial solution we point it out, whether the solution is found in one of our tests or in others.

We believe that much research is needed on critical thinking testing, but this is true of all educational testing. Our view is, however, that (with some specific limitations that we cite) the commercially available critical thinking tests have been carefully developed and are likely to serve you better than hastily constructed instruments.

Guidelines for Examining Tests

On the opposite page are seven guidelines we suggest for examining critical thinking tests, be they commercially available ones or those you make yourself. They provide a way to think systematically about tests.

Note that in choosing and using a critical thinking test, the user must take a large part of the responsibility for deciding whether the test is suitable for the intended purpose. Since no test is suitable for all purposes, the user must make a conscious assessment of suitability to his or her current situation.

It would be very helpful if, when reading our comments about a given test, you have a copy of the test on hand. Information for obtaining the various tests is given in the annotated list at the end of this chapter.

SEVEN GUIDELINES FOR EXAMINING TESTS

1. Pay close attention to the directions, the items, and the scoring guide.

2. Take the test yourself, and compare your answers with those of the guide.

3. Satisfy yourself that the scoring guide is reasonable, but do not expect to agree with it completely for any but deduction items.

4. Ask yourself often, "Does this really test for some aspect of critical thinking?"

5. For purported comprehensive critical thinking tests, ask yourself, "Does this cover enough of critical thinking in a balanced manner to be called a comprehensive critical thinking test?"

6. For purported aspect-specific critical thinking tests, ask yourself, "Does this cover enough of the aspect?"

7. Read the test manual and note the statistical information, but remember that test publishers have a conflict of interest in deciding what information to include and exclude, and remember our warnings in chapter 2 about information on reliability.

Section One: Comprehensive Critical Thinking Tests

To our knowledge there are eight commercially available comprehensive critical thinking tests, all but one of which are based on general knowledge (Test of Enquiry Skills being a borderline case):

- Watson-Glaser Critical Thinking Appraisal
- Cornell Critical Thinking Test, Level X
- Cornell Critical Thinking Test, Level Z
- Ross Test of Higher Cognitive Processes
- New Jersey Test of Reasoning Skills
- Judgment: Deductive Logic and Assumption Recognition
- Test of Enquiry Skills
- The Ennis-Weir Critical Thinking Essay Test

We shall describe each test briefly and comment on sample items. This will give you a flavor for each test, show some general problems in critical thinking testing, and exhibit actual attempts to test for major aspects of critical thinking.

1. Watson-Glaser Critical Thinking Appraisal

The multiple-choice Watson-Glaser test, first developed in the late 1930's, has been around the longest. Through its various revisions it is probably the most extensively used critical thinking test, so it is a bench mark against which others must be compared. There are two parallel forms of the Watson-Glaser test, and each form is supposed to test for the same aspects of critical thinking. The primary audience for the test is high school and college level students, but the test can be used at the junior high level. Each form contains 80 multiple-choice items divided into five subtests as shown in table 3.1.

Guideline 5 suggests that you ask whether the test covers enough of critical thinking in a balanced manner. Our answer to this question is basically affirmative, even though the test does not attend to the credibility of sources and observations, the semantic aspects of critical thinking, or critical thinking dispositions.

The Inference subtest is designed to test whether the examinee has the ability for judging the likelihood, given certain evidence, of a conclusion being true or false. Examinees are presented with passages containing information on different topics, and they are

---

Table 3.1. Watson-Glaser
Critical Thinking Appraisal:
Five Subtests

Inference

Recognition of Assumptions

Deduction

Interpretation

Evaluation of Arguments

---

instructed to regard the information in the passages as true. After each passage are several items. Each item is a conclusion that someone might draw from the information in the passage. Examinees are to decide for each conclusion whether it is true, probably true, false, probably false, or without sufficient information for a decision. Here is an example from Form A:

> Mr. Brown, who lives in the town of Salem, was brought before the Salem municipal court for the sixth time in the past month on a charge of keeping his pool hall open after 1 a.m. He again admitted his guilt and was fined the maximum, $500, as in each earlier instance.
>
> 6. On some nights it was to Mr. Brown's advantage to keep his pool hall open after 1 a.m., even at the risk of paying a $500 fine.

In accord with guideline 2, stop for a moment and decide on your answer: True, Probably True, Insufficient Data, Probably False, or False.

The key says item 6 is "Probably True." But if you consider the item for a while, in line with guideline 3, you will probably think of other possible explanations of the information given in the situation's description. For example, Mr. Brown might have suffered a severe personal loss a month earlier and had commenced heavy drinking, resulting in his losing control of the pool hall. Or Mr. Brown might have turned over the pool hall to his son to whom he gave a free hand, to make up for neglecting him as a child. Or perhaps Mr. Brown was engaged in civil disobedience. We could go on and on. In each case it might well have been false that it was to Brown's advantage to keep his pool hall open after 1 a.m.

The number of such alternatives that occurs to someone depends at least on the person's knowledge about such situations, the person's creativity and interest, and the amount of time that the person spends on the item. A sophisticated and experienced person might well stop to think of a variety of such alternatives, or might just realize from experience that there are no doubt many other possible explanations of the information given. To the extent that such thinking occurs, the person is justified in selecting "Insufficient Data."

Basically, problems can occur for inductive inference items such as this one because examinees have different background beliefs and different levels of sophistication. These problems are not limited to the Watson-Glaser test. They exist for all multiple-choice inductive inference items with which we are familiar, including those on our own tests, and many other types of items as well.

In the next chapter we shall suggest some ways for reducing these problems, but you should not expect the best critical thinkers to agree perfectly with the keyed answers on multiple-choice critical thinking tests. We also suggest that you use the key provided with a test for students whose background beliefs and level of sophistication fit that key. Otherwise, fashion a new key that fits your students, but realize that the norms provided in the manual would not then be applicable.

The second section of the Watson-Glaser test examines the ability to recognize unstated assumptions or presuppositions in what people say. Examinees are presented a number of statements in which certain things are taken for granted. After each statement there are some proposed assumptions. The task is to decide for each proposed assumption whether or not it was necessarily taken for granted in the original statement. Examples of assumption-identification items will be examined in chapter 4.

The third subtest is on deductive reasoning. Examinees are presented a short paragraph and several possible conclusions from that paragraph. They are to decide for each conclusion whether or not it necessarily follows from the statements in the paragraph. Examples of deduction items will be examined in chapter 4.

The fourth subtest is entitled Interpretation. Its items test for the ability to weigh evidence and to decide whether proposed conclusions *follow beyond a reasonable doubt* from the evidence (another task that depends on background beliefs and level of sophistication). This task differs from the deductive reasoning section, where the task is to decide whether or not conclusions follow *necessarily* from given information.

The fifth section of the Watson-Glaser test examines the ability to differentiate strong lines of reasoning from those that are weak. Examinees are presented with a series of questions about important issues. After each question there is a set of answers. The answers respond either affirmatively or negatively to the original question and then provide reasons for that response. Examinees are to accept the reasons provided as true and to decide, on the assumption that the reasons are true, whether they provide strong or weak support for the response to the question. Here is an example:

> Would a strong labor party promote the general welfare of the people of the United States?
>
> 67. No; labor unions have called strikes in a number of important industries.

In accord with guideline 2 and guideline 3, we invite you to stop to judge whether the reason given in item 67 is strong or weak.

Item 67 is keyed "Weak." However, someone with a conservative ideology might understandably judge the reason to be strong. This possibility reveals another danger in critical thinking testing—that of testing for a student's political views or ideology. Further, it leads us to question whether this section satisfies guideline 4. Does it really test for some aspect of critical thinking, or is it too ideologically based to do so?

Reliability estimates for the Watson-Glaser range from .70 to .82, consistent with the range for other multiple-choice critical thinking tests. Information on the test's validity includes studies which show increases in test performance following instruction in critical thinking, and correlations of the test with measures of general intelligence, aptitude, and achievement.

The Watson-Glaser test is important for its long history. There exists a large body of data and research using the Watson-Glaser which can serve as part of the basis for comparing students' current critical thinking performance.

2 and 3. Cornell Critical Thinking Tests

There are two Cornell critical thinking tests, Level X and Level Z, sharing a common manual. They are aimed at different educational levels and do not cover exactly the same aspects of critical thinking. Level X is the easier, and it is intended primarily for junior and senior high school and first year college, but has been used in grades four through six. Level Z is meant to be used for undergraduates, graduate students, and adults. However, the ability level of examinees and their backgrounds in critical thinking should also be taken into account in making a choice. The above broad recommendations assume that the students have had little instruction in critical thinking and that they have average ability for the groups mentioned.

Like all multiple-choice critical thinking tests, these tests focus primarily on the evaluative aspects of critical thinking rather than the productive aspects discussed in chapter 1. For example, the tests examine whether students can judge the reliability of reports of observations which other people have made, but they do not examine whether the students can themselves make reliable observations.

The manual for the tests characterizes a critical thinker as having proficiency in judging whether

1. a statement follows from the premises;

2. something is an assumption;

3. an observation statement is reliable;

4. an alleged authority is reliable;

5. a simple generalization is warranted;

6. a hypothesis is warranted;

7. a theory is warranted;

8. an argument depends on an ambiguity;

9. a statement is overly vague or overly specific;

10. a reason is relevant.

Of the ten proficiencies listed, Level X covers all except 7, 8, and 9. Level Z covers all except 7, but gives less emphasis than Level X to 3 and 4. Applying our guideline 5, we judge these tests to be comprehensive enough to be called critical thinking tests, although, in addition to the limitations just noted, they do not attend to critical thinking dispositions.

Level X. In Level X, there are 71 multiple-choice items (not counting the example items) divided into four sections (cf. table 3.2).

The context is a story about a group of explorers from Earth who have just landed on the newly discovered planet, Nicoma. The explorers are on Nicoma to search for another group of explorers who were the first to land on Nicoma two years earlier.

Table 3.2. Cornell Critical Thinking Test,
Level X: Four Sections

Inductive Inference

Credibility of Sources and Observation

Deduction

Assumption Identification

Examinees are asked to imagine that they are members of the search party.

The task in Section I (Inductive Inference) is to determine whether pieces of information discovered by the search party are (1) evidence for, (2) evidence against, or (3) neither evidence for nor against the idea that the members of the first group are all dead. Like the Inference section of the Watson-Glaser test, justifiable answers depend to some extent on one's background beliefs and one's level of sophistication. Thus, accommodations similar to those recommended earlier are required for different student populations.

In Section II (Credibility of Sources and Observations), statements made by members of the search party are presented in pairs, and examinees are asked to judge which, if either, of the statements is more believable. Here is an example:

    27A.   The health officer says, "This water is safe to drink."

      B.   Several others are soldiers. One of them says, "This water supply is not safe."

      C.   A and B are equally believable.

What answer do you choose?

The key says **A**, but one's background beliefs might justifiably lead to a different answer. Suppose that one believed that health officers are paid political hacks, but that soldiers are well trained to judge the quality of water supplies. Then one might be justified in choosing **B** as the answer. On the other hand, one might believe that soldiers and health officers are equally well trained to judge water quality, in which case one might justifiably choose answer **C**.

In Section III (Deduction) the explorers are reasoning about what to do and what to expect. In each case examinees are asked to choose which of three possibilities follows from the information given. That is, they are asked to "suppose that what the person says is true," and then to choose "what else would have to be true" from among three alternatives. Since these deductive inference questions admit of only one correct answer, this section is much less likely to depend on examinees' background knowledge and level of sophistication. As we mentioned previously, types of deduction items will be considered in chapter 4.

In Section IV (Identifying Assumptions), the task is to say what is probably taken for granted in the reasoning of characters in the story. We shall have several suggestions about assumption-identification items in chapter 4.

Level Z. Level Z has 52 multiple-choice items, 19 fewer than Level X, and seven sections, three more than Level X. The result is that some sections have a small number of items, probably making it unwise to rely on section scores for judging individual student's performance. Average section scores for groups might well be all right. (See table 3.3 for the names of the seven sections in Level Z.)

Section I is on deductive reasoning, but it adds the complication of incorporating emotionally loaded language and propositions. The first five items of the section are cast in the context of two men debating whether eighteen-year-olds should be permitted to vote, and the second five are in the context of the men

Table 3.3. Cornell Critical Thinking Test,
Level Z: Seven Sections

Deduction

Meaning

Credibility

Inductive Inference (direction of support, if any)

Inductive Inference (prediction and hypothesis testing)

Definition and Unstated Reasons

Assumption Identification

debating immigration policies. The task is to decide whether, for each item, the proposed conclusions (1) follow necessarily from the reasons given; (2) contradict the reasons given; or (3) neither. This task is more difficult than the deduction tasks of Level X, in which examinees were asked only to choose which of three possibilities follows from the information given. In Level Z they must make a decision about each proposed conclusion. So Level Z represents two steps up in difficulty over Level X. It uses emotionally loaded situations and requires an absolute rather than a comparative decision about each proposition.

Section II focuses on the linguistic strategies and tactics required for interacting with other people in a problem situation. This topic is not included in the Level X at all. Examinees are presented with a discussion about whether the water supply of a town ought to be chlorinated. After each short episode of the discussion, the task is to select from options provided the best reasons why the thinking in the episode is faulty.

Sections III, IV, and V refer to an experiment conducted to see what happens to ducklings that eat cabbage worms. Section

III deals with the credibility of statements from different sources. Examinees are asked in each item to judge which, if either, of two statements is more believable. Section IV requires examinees to judge whether particular pieces of information support, go against, or neither support nor go against the conclusion that cabbage worms are poisonous to ducklings. Thus, Sections III and IV are comparable in form to the credibility and inductive inference sections of Level X, and, accordingly, keyed answers do assume a common set of background beliefs and a moderate level of sophistication.

Section V is on prediction and hypothesis testing. It asks examinees to judge the utility of various predictions in testing the hypothesis that ducklings will die within six hours after eating a cabbage worm. Seven possible predictions are provided for consideration. Each item asks examinees to look at three of the seven predictions and to judge which of the three is best for guiding an experiment. Here is an example:

42. Of n, o, and p, which is the best prediction?

n. If one Mallard duckling is selected at random from each of six different broods, and each selected duckling is fed a cabbage worm, all six ducklings will be dead within six hours.

o. Suppose twelve hungry, randomly selected Canvasback ducklings are turned loose for one hour in a cabbage patch containing worms and then put in a clean cage for six hours. If each dies during that period, the results of the stomach tests will show that each has eaten a cabbage worm.

p. If a group of ten healthy Canvasback ducklings that would probably live if not fed cabbage worms is randomly split in half, and each half is treated the same except that one group of five eats cabbage worms, then the worm-fed ducklings will die within six hours and the other ducklings probably will not.

In accord with our guideline 2, decide for yourself which prediction you prefer.

The keyed answer for item 42 is that prediction **p** is the best of the three. Apply guideline 3 and judge whether you accept the reasons for this choice. Prediction **p** is better than **o** because **o** is not implied by the hypothesis being tested. It is better than **n** because **p** provides a control group, which **n** does not. These items require careful reading if the task is to be understood. Applying guideline 4, they do appear to test for critical thinking at a sophisticated level.

Section VI of Level Z contains items on definitions and unstated reasons or beliefs. The items require fairly sophisticated thinking, and there are no similar items on Level X. Each item presents a discussion in which a person questions the meaning of some word or expression as used by another person in the discussion. Examinees are to select from the alternatives the definition that best suits what is said by the person being questioned. Item 45 contains a discussion between Mary and her father about what she is making. The father thinks she is making something from dough but Mary disagrees, so the father wonders what she means by "dough."

45. "What are you making with that dough?" asked Mary's father.

"Dough!" exclaimed Mary. "Did you ever see anything made with yeast that was baked immediately after it was mixed? Naturally not," she said as she put the mixture into the oven immediately after mixing it. "Therefore, it's not dough."

"What do *you* mean by 'dough'?" her father asked.

Of the following, which is the best way to state *Mary's* notion of dough?

A. Dough is a mixture of flour and other ingredients, including yeast.

B. Dough is a mixture of flour and other ingredients, not baked immediately.

    C.   Dough is a mixture of flour and other
           ingredients, often baked in an oven.

In accord with our guidelines 1 to 4, we invite you to do the item and judge whether you think that it tests for some aspect of critical thinking. The keyed answer is **A**.

Section VII presents reasoning based on assumptions. Examinees are to choose from three alternatives the statement that is most probably the unstated assumption. We will not illustrate this section here, but we shall discuss assumption-identification items in chapter 4.

Although recently republished, the Cornell tests have a history of use which extends back to the late fifties and early sixties. For this reason the authors have been able to provide a variety of norms in the manual. Given its history, the test can serve, along with the Watson-Glaser test, as a bench mark for comparing critical thinking performance across different groups and over time.

Reliability estimates for Level X range from .67 to .90, and for Level Z range from .50 to .77. The information contained in the manual on the validity of the tests is fairly extensive. There is a discussion of the extent to which the tests cover an appropriate selection of critical thinking content. In addition, there is a report of the empirical research which has been done on the tests, including correlations of the tests with other variables, factor analyses of the test scores, and results of experimental studies of critical thinking. The authors suggest that interpretation of some of this information is not clear, so they provide suggestions and invite test users to think through the issues themselves.

4. Ross Test of Higher Cognitive Processes

The Ross test is aimed at students in grades four through six and is designed to test students' ability to analyze, synthesize, and evaluate. These activities comprise the upper three levels of Bloom's Taxonomy of Educational Objectives. The test consists of 105 multiple-choice items, requiring two sittings of about an hour apiece. Sections 1 through 5 are given in the first sitting.

There are a number of suggested uses, including screening, assessing program effectiveness, and assessing individual students. The test sections can be seen in table 3.4.

It is not clear why the sections of the test correspond to Bloom's taxonomy in the way that the authors claim: Analysis is supposed to correspond to Sections I, III, and VII; Synthesis to Sections IV, V, and VIII; and Evaluation to Sections II and VI. It seems, rather, that analysis, synthesis, and evaluation are assessed by all sections. To some extent, this problem arises from the vagueness and overlap in the Bloom categories themselves. We concur with the discussion in volume 1 that the categories are too vague to provide clear guidance to instruction. Neither can they provide clear guidance to evaluation. Note, however, that Bloom did not say that his categories were intended to serve either of these guidance roles.

In the following discussion, we shall apply our guidelines 4 and 5 that deal with whether parts of the test really test for critical

Table 3. 4. Ross Test of
Higher Cognitive Processes:
Eight Sections

I.	Analogies
II.	Deductive Reasoning
III.	Missing Premises
IV.	Abstract Relations
V.	Sequential Synthesis
VI.	Questioning Strategies
VII.	Analysis of Relevant and Irrelevant Information
VIII.	Analysis of Attributes

thinking and whether the test covers enough of critical thinking to be called a comprehensive critical thinking test.

Since this test is called a "cognitive processes" test, it should not be surprising—and not taken as a criticism of the test—that it contains categories that do not appear to be critical thinking and provides minimal coverage of some aspects of critical thinking. We include it in our listing of critical thinking tests because there are so few critical thinking tests, and because it does include some sections that are clearly critical thinking and some sections that are closely related. Sections that clearly test for critical thinking are Deductive Reasoning and Missing Premises. Section VII, dealing with relevant information, is also clearly critical thinking, although its content is specific to mathematics. Section VIII requires inductive inference, but it seems to be borderline critical thinking because the content—complex stick figures—is artificial compared to that used in typical inductive inference. However, this is a matter of judgment and further research.

Sections I and V, Analogies and Sequential Synthesis, do seem to require critical thinking, but we hesitate to include them in the mainstream of critical thinking. We have the same hesitation with Section IV, Abstract Relations, in which examinees are asked to figure out just what the test maker sees in common among a set of given words. These three sections (I, IV, and V) seem to be similar to the sorts of things found in IQ tests.

Section VI, Questioning Strategies, seems mislabeled. Examinees are not asked to exhibit questioning strategies, nor to judge what strategy should be most helpful. Rather, they are asked to interpret answers to sets of questions developed by the test writers and to judge which set of questions was most helpful in identifying which of a group of several items is "IT." A real questioning strategies section would certainly be desirable in a comprehensive critical thinking test. None of the other tests, however, comes even this close.

In Section II, Deductive Reasoning, students are given some statements which they are to assume to be true and a number of possible conclusions from those statements. The task is to decide whether or not the conclusions follow from the given statements. This is an example:

> All palimons are known to be fish eaters.
> Palimons are also migratory creatures.
> Therefore,
> 18. All fish eaters are palimons.
>   A. conclusion follows
>   B. conclusion does not follow

There are no such things as palimons; and "fish eaters" is a stilted way to speak. Thus the content is abstract. We realize that an advantage of the abstractness is that it provides a check on the verbal flexibility of the examinee and might also lessen the influence of background knowledge. You must decide whether or not this abstract flavor detracts from its being a critical thinking test. Reasonable people can differ about this point.

We shall provide an example from Section VI, Abstract Relationships, to show why we do not think that this section is central to a test of critical thinking. The task requires students to examine four provided words and to choose from a provided pool of other words one which goes with all of the first four words "in some way." Try to do the following example before reading on to see the keyed answer:

42. hair   class   short   throat

```
┌─────────────────────────────┐
│          Word Pool I        │
│                             │
│   A.  pin       G.  line    │
│   B.  shoe      H.  cross   │
│   C.  green     I.  sign    │
│   D.  red       J.  true    │
│   E.  cut       K.  market  │
│   F.  saw       L.  horse   │
│                             │
└─────────────────────────────┘
```

The keyed answer is that **E**, the word "cut," goes with all four words: haircut, cut class, shortcut, cutthroat. Unfortunately, several other words from the word pool also go with all four of the item words. Be that as it may, this kind of activity, though perhaps a test of language familiarity and quick-mindedness, does not seem to be central to deciding what to believe or do in the kind of real situations where we want students to think critically.

We feel that the Ross test is too much like IQ tests to serve as a standard critical thinking test, but the authors present evidence of low correlations between the Ross test and the Lorge-Thorndike IQ test; so, maybe our intuitions are inaccurate. No doubt it would give some indication of a student's critical thinking ability. What do you think, given our brief description of the test? Better still, and in accord with our first five guidelines, take the test yourself and decide what you think.

Statistical information for the Ross test was determined using samples of gifted and non-gifted students. Reliability estimates are high for a critical thinking test; they are reported as .92 for split-half and .94 for test-retest. The high reliability can probably be explained by a number of factors:

1. the large number of items (105) and generous amount of testing time;

2. the heavy use of deductive reasoning, which usually provides the most consistent answers on critical thinking tests;

3. the use of abstract content about which students do not have differences in background beliefs; and

4. the similarity of some sections to sections of intelligence tests which, as has been already mentioned, tend to have higher reliabilities than critical thinking tests.

Information offered in support of the validity of the test includes a correlation of .67 between total score on the test and chronological age. Since critical thinking ought to increase with age, this correlation provides evidence in favor of the test. Other information includes the facts that gifted students do better on the test than students who are not gifted, and that performance on the test was not highly related to scores on the Lorge-Thorndike intelligence test in two reported instances. The authors suggest that these are findings that should be expected if the test is valid.

5. New Jersey Test of Reasoning Skills

New Jersey Test of Reasoning Skills seems to have been constructed specifically for use with the Philosophy for Children program devised by the Institute for the Advancement of Philosophy for Children. However, the test could be used in other contexts. The manual recommends that the test can be used with students at the fifth grade level and more mature individuals, apparently including secondary and college students. Obviously, with such a wide range there are likely to be problems suiting the interests, reading levels, and thinking ability levels of everyone in the range. The authors caution that the test may be seen as juvenile by examinees at the older end of the range. There are similar problems with the Watson-Glaser and the Cornell Level X tests, but probably they are not as pronounced with those instruments.

The test is designed to test "reasoning in language" and is not actually called a critical thinking test. As with the Ross test we have included it in our list because it covers enough critical thinking content that it should be known to anyone interested in choosing a critical thinking test. Twenty-two skill areas are covered in the test, including those listed in table 3.5.

The test contains 50 multiple-choice items. Given the number of skill areas tested, you can see that on the average there can be about two items per skill. An inspection of the items, however, shows that about half the items are concerned with deduction. This heavy emphasis on deduction diminishes, but certainly does not destroy, its usefulness as a comprehensive critical thinking test. Deduction is an essential part of critical thinking, but probably not half of it.

Table 3.5. New Jersey Test of
Reasoning Skills:
Ten (of Twenty-two) Skill Areas

Translating into logical form
Recognizing improper questions
Avoiding jumping to conclusions
Analogical reasoning
Detecting underlying assumptions
Detecting ambiguities
Discerning causal relationships
Identifying good reasons
Distinguishing differences of kind
    and degree
Recognizing transitive relationships

An answer key is not provided. Rather, some free test scoring
is provided for those who buy copies of the test.

The following example is designed to test for examinees'
ability to see when someone is jumping to a conclusion:

5. "I know a girl from France who's very tall," said Pete.

    "Then everyone from France must be tall," replied Joe.

    Joe's reply is:

    a. good reasoning, because people from the
       same country are very much alike.

    b. poor reasoning, because people from the
       same country are often different.

    c. poor reasoning, because only people who have
       been to France know if everyone there is tall.

Presumably the keyed answer is **b,** but we can see how even this simple item depends on background beliefs. In this case, an examinee needs to believe that people from the same country are often different. We do not know whether this belief is prevalent among the audience for whom the test was made.

Table 3.6. New Jersey Test of Reasoning Skills
Major Subheadings Under Reasoning Skills Category

Seeking criteria for cognitive inquiry
Ordering and sorting
Discerning relationships
Inferring as figuring things out
Skills of reasonable discussion

The reported reliability indexes range from .85 for fifth grade students to .91 for seventh grade. The primary evidence for the test's validity rests on how well the test items cover a representative sample of the content of "reasoning in language." The test is based upon an extensive taxonomy which is divided into two major classes, Reasoning Skills and Inquiry Skills. The idea is that the test should be valid to the extent that the taxonomy is complete, and that the test covers the taxonomy. The major headings under the Reasoning Skills category are listed in table 3.6. Each of these headings is subdivided into other categories. The major headings under the Inquiry Skills category are listed in table 3.7.

Overall it seems that the New Jersey test is a relatively unexplored instrument with simple content and a heavy emphasis on deduction.

Table 3.7. New Jersey Test of Reasoning Skills
Major Subheadings Under Inquiry Skills Category

Criteria of acceptable inquiry

Problem solving and decision making

Describing

Providing causal explanations

Seeking, finding, and employing evidence

Reasoning inductively

Constructing hypotheses and making
predictions

Considering consequences

Estimating

6. Judgment: Deductive Logic
And Assumption Recognition

Although the title of this test from Instructional Objectives Exchange specifically mentions only two aspects of critical thinking, the test also includes a ten-item section on the credibility of sources and observations. These three aspects are central to critical thinking, so we group the test with comprehensive critical thinking tests, even though it does not test, among other things, induction and critical thinking dispositions.

The test has 48 items based on general knowledge. It can be given in 40 minutes and is aimed at students in grades 7-12. It is deemed to be a criterion-referenced test, but no standard of satisfactory performance required by criterion-referenced tests is supplied as a basis for judgment. The discussion of criterion-referenced and norm-referenced testing in chapter 4 will make this point clearer.

Unfortunately, there is little information provided about this test. However, its greater use could result in information about levels of success for various grade levels and about such questions as the relationships between scores on the emotionally loaded items and open-mindedness as judged by an impartial observer. We shall comment only about the deduction section.

The deduction section includes some items with emotionally loaded content. This is a desirable feature because it might be a partial measure of the disposition to be open-minded.

Some test users will be unhappy with the way the deduction questions are asked. Item 16 from the class reasoning section provides an example:

16.   Given:

All conscientious objectors are draft dodgers.

All draft dodgers are cowards.

Then, would this conclusion be valid?

All conscientious objectors are cowards.

How would you answer the question? How do you think that a logically unsophisticated liberal student would answer?

In the area of deduction, validity is applied to *the strength* of reasoning, but not to conclusions, as item 16 suggests. Reasoning is deductively valid if it would be a contradiction to deny its conclusion once you have accepted its premises. Item 16 thus contains deductively valid reasoning. *If* you accept the premises, you must accept the conclusion, or else contradict yourself. On this account of validity, you can regard the reasoning as valid, even if you do not regard its conclusion or its premises as *true*. It is this technical notion of "valid," applied to reasoning strength, which is the basis of deduction. However, in this test the question requires that the valid thing be a *conclusion*, because the question specifically asks about the conclusion. There is thus a risk of confusing examinees who have learned the standard deductive reasoning distinction between the validity of reasoning and the truth or falsity of the premises and conclusion.

This neglected test, because of its simplicity and ease of scoring, might well be more heavily used. We hope that the authors remedy the problem with the word "valid."

7. Test of Enquiry Skills

The Enquiry Skills test was developed for students in grades 7-10 in Australia. These might not be the most appropriate grade levels for North American use, so we suggest that you examine the content. It contains 87 items divided approximately evenly among the three sections given in table 3.8.

Parts A and B focus on the school subjects of science and social science, while Part C is focused on science alone. Thus Part C, if it were a separate test, would be a subject-specific critical thinking test. The manual does not provide a separate reliability estimate for Part C, though it does give estimates for each section in Part C (.70, .66, and .67). Other sections have test-retest reliability estimates ranging from .65 to .82. Thus, separate section scores can probably be trusted for groups of students, though not for individuals except on a very tentative basis.

Here is an example of an induction item from the Enquiry Skills test:

75. Mary wanted to find out if something in the air caused boiled milk to go sour. To investigate this, she carried out the following steps:

    She boiled a container filled with milk.

    She left the boiled milk without a lid for 10 minutes.

    She then put the lid on the container of boiled milk.

    She left the container untouched in a cupboard for a week.

    After a week she observed that the milk had gone sour.

In order to conclude that something in the air had caused the milk to go sour, Mary would also need

A. a container of boiled milk that had its lid put on as soon as the milk boiled.

B. a container of unboiled milk with its lid on.

C. a container of boiled milk that was left without its lid for the whole week.

D. an empty container with its lid off.

E. a container of milk that was already sour with its lid on.

The keyed answer is **A**. The selection of this answer presupposes some understanding of the relationship between boiling milk and the souring of milk, an understanding that some students will not have. So the background knowledge issue arises for this test also.

This test deviates significantly from the definition of critical thinking that we presented in chapter 1, since there are no assumption-identification or credibility sections, and only three deduction items. On the other hand, it does test for induction in Sections 8 and 9, albeit with science content which some students will not understand. In addition, it places more emphasis on the gathering and interpretation of information in Sections 1 to 6 than most other critical thinking tests. Applying our guideline 5, we judge this test to contain enough critical thinking content to be grouped with the comprehensive critical thinking tests, but we are concerned about the neglect of deduction, assumption identification, and credibility.

Since the topics not covered by the Enquiry Skills test are included in the Judgment test that we just discussed, one possibility would be to give a combination of the Enquiry Skills test and the Judgment test. This would still neglect testing for the critical thinking dispositions, but no multiple-choice tests do that to any significant extent.

Table 3.8. Test of Enquiry Skills
Three Sections with Subsections

Part A—Using Reference Materials
    1. Library usage
    2. Index and table of contents
Part B—Interpretating and Processing Information
    3. Scales
    4. Averages, percentages, and proportions
    5. Charts and tables
    6. Graphs
Part C—Critical Thinking in Science
    7. Comprehension of science reading
    8. Designs of experimental procedures
    9. Conclusions and generalizations

8. The Ennis-Weir Critical Thinking Essay Test

The Ennis-Weir test is the only commercially available, comprehensive critical thinking test in essay format. The test is aimed primarily at high school and college students, but it has been used with some success with students as low as sixth grade. The test is unique in that it tests for some critical thinking dispositions. Some of the areas of critical thinking which are examined by the test are shown in table 3.9.

Examinees are given a fictitious letter to the editor of the Moorburg newspaper. The letter contains eight numbered paragraphs in which the letter writer argues that overnight parking on city streets in Moorburg should be eliminated. The task is to respond to the letter by writing an evaluation of the thinking in

Table 3.9. The Ennis-Weir Critical Thinking
Essay Test: Representative Areas of
Critical Thinking Examined by the Test

Getting the point

Seeing the reasons and assumptions

Stating one's point

Offering good reasons

Seeing other possibilities (including other possible
explanations)

Responding appropriately to and/or avoiding:
Equivocation

Irrelevance

Circularity

Reversal of an "if-then" (or other
conditional) relationship

The straw person fallacy

Overgeneralization

Excessive skepticism

Credibility problems

The use of emotive language to persuade

each of the letter writer's eight paragraphs and an evaluation of the thinking in the letter as a whole.

The manual for the test provides a detailed description of the sorts of responses students might give and of how they should be scored. Once the manual is understood, students' responses are fairly easy to score and, with practice, each response can be scored in fewer than ten minutes. The authors state that they can grade each response in six minutes, or about ten per hour. Note that a machine that scores multiple-choice tests at ten thousand per hour operates a thousand times as fast, a significant economic fact that is offered in response to complaints about multiple-choice tests.

We will present a key part of the directions, the first part of the letter, and a summary of the directions for scoring an examinee's response to that part. Some other parts of the letter appear in chapter 1 and were used when we discussed the definition of critical thinking.

> For each paragraph in the letter below, write a paragraph in reply telling whether you believe the thinking to be good or bad. *Defend your judgments with reasons.*
>
> Dear Editor:
>
> Overnight parking on all streets in Moorburg should be eliminated. To achieve this goal, parking should be prohibited from 2 a.m. to 6 a.m. There are a number of reasons why any intelligent citizen should agree.
> 1. For one thing, to park overnight is to have a garage in the streets. Now it is illegal for anyone to have a garage in the city streets. Clearly, then, it should be against the law to park overnight in the streets.

The manual states that the letter writer's thinking in this first paragraph is weak because the analogy between parking and having a garage in the streets is weak. It instructs the grader to give examinees the maximum credit allowed (3 points) for any of the following:

(1)   pointing out the inappropriateness of the analogy;

(2)   indicating the incorrectness of the definition of "garage";

(3)   specifying ways in which parking a car in the streets is different from having a garage there; or

(4)   indicating the shift in meaning with the word "garage."

Some students will rate the letter writer's thinking as poor because he has failed to indicate where the people might park if they are not allowed to park in the streets. This is judged to be a weak answer because it does not directly address the argument of the paragraph.

Graders have leeway to give a student full credit for good thinking that was not foreseen by the test's authors and described in the manual. Hence, flexibility is provided for handling varying levels of sophistication and varying background beliefs among examinees, significantly reducing a problem that haunts multiple-choice testing of critical thinking. On the other hand, critical thinking and flexibility must be exercised by graders, and these are not always easy tasks. In addition, as indicated before, grading the essay test takes more time.

As noted in chapter 2, it is often impossible to get estimates of the reliability of essay tests by splitting them into parts and correlating performance on the parts. The reliability estimates reported for the Ennis-Weir test are based upon interrater comparisons. The estimates given are .86 and .82, which are relatively high for essay tests. However, these numbers only mean that different graders tend to rank students the same, not that they tend to give about the same level of score. Different graders may rank examinees' responses in the same order, but still have widely different average scores. For instance, two graders might rate the same three students as in table 3.10.

According to both graders, Student C scored the best, Student B next, and Student A the worst. But according to Grader 1, the three students did much worse than according to Grader 2. Therefore, the two graders would likely make different judgments about the students' critical thinking. This is a potential problem with the test that has not been sufficiently explored.

Justification for the test's validity is based primarily on the fact that the test presents examinees with a typical real-life situation in which critical thinking is needed and asks them to reason

Table 3.10. Hypothetical Ratings of Three Students by Two Graders on the Ennis-Weir Test

| | Student | | |
	A	B	C
Grader 1	5	7	9
Grader 2	15	17	19

soundly about a representative range of moves that people make when trying to persuade each other.

Section Two: Aspect-specific Critical Thinking Tests

There are four commercially available, aspect-specific critical thinking tests. Three of these are in the area of deductive thinking, and the other examines ability to appraise statements of observation:

- Cornell Class Reasoning Test, Form X
- Cornell Conditional Reasoning Test, Form X
- Logical Reasoning
- Test on Appraising Observations

As with the comprehensive critical thinking tests, we will describe each test briefly and comment on sample items.

1. Cornell Class Reasoning Test, Form X

This test is designed for use in fourth through twelfth grade. It is not timed, but can be done by upper secondary students within a class period. For the youngest students, two sittings are probably desirable. A correction formula to take account of guessing is suggested in which total score would equal the number of items answered correctly minus one-half of those answered incorrectly.

The test contains 72 multiple-choice items which examine twelve principles of class logic, each with six items. Varying types of content are used for the items. The six items in each group consist of four items whose content is concrete and familiar; that is, the content used is concrete articles having qualities with which examinees have been associated. An example would be the statement "Many cats are black." One item in each group of six contains symbolic content, meaning that symbols such as "x," "y," and "A" are used. An example is, "All A's are B's." Finally, one item with suggestive content is included in each group of six. With suggestive content examinees are asked to assume for the purposes of reasoning the truth of obviously false premises.

The following item uses concrete familiar content:

7. Suppose you know that

> All the cars in the garage are Mr. Smith's.

> All Mr. Smith's cars are Fords.

Then would this be true?

All of the cars in the garage are Fords.

> A. Yes, it must be true

> B. No, it can't be true

> C. Maybe, it may be true or it may not be true

The keyed answer is **A**: it must be true that all the cars in the garage are Fords. This type of deduction is called "class reasoning" because it depends on stated relationships between classes or groups of things: *cars in the garage* and *Mr. Smith's cars*.

Here is another example that has similar form, but uses symbolic content.

19. Suppose you know that

All Z's are Y's

All Y's are X's

Then would this be true?

All Z's are X's

   A. Yes, it must be true

   B. No, it can't be true

   C. Maybe, it may be true or it may not be true

The keyed answer is again **A**, it must be true that all Z's are X's.

Finally, here is an item of similar form, but using suggestive content.

31. Suppose you know that

All cats can fly.

All animals that can fly are black.

Then would this be true?

All cats are black.

   A. Yes, it must be true

   B. No, it can't be true

   C. Maybe, it may be true or it may not be true

The answer is again **A**: it must be true that all cats are black. In this latter item the thinking required is different from the previous two examples. Here examinees are asked first to assume things which they know are not true, namely, that all cats can fly and that all animals that can fly are black. Having assumed these things, they then must accept as true for the purposes of the example a conclusion which they know is false. The value of the item is that often it is necessary to assume, for the purposes of present argument, things which we believe to be false to see where they lead. This item measures students' ability to separate the *form* of reasoning from its *content*. It differs from Item 16 of the Judgment test discussed previously, because of the explicit direction to suppose true what is known to be false.

Since the content used in this test is sometimes unrealistic and abstract, the test's directness as a practical measure of this aspect of critical thinking is diminished unless we make the assumption that what is measured transfers to practical situations. On the other hand, it does seem plausible that if someone cannot reason from a premise such as "All cats can fly," then the person will have difficulty reasoning from more practical things that he or she does not believe.

The reliability of the test was estimated by correlating the scores on two administrations of the test given approximately ten weeks apart. The values ranged from .66 to .88. Content validity of the test was established by examining the field of logic and specific examples of logical reasoning, including newspaper editorials, court opinions, and a handbook for auto mechanics, and by securing endorsement from specialists in deductive logic. Total test score is also correlated with chronological age and uncorrelated with sex. If it is assumed that logical reasoning increases with age and is unrelated to a person's sex, then these figures support the validity.

2. Cornell Conditional Reasoning Test, Form X

This test has the same structure as the previous one. It contains 72 multiple-choice items, divided into twelve groups, each testing a different logical principle. The content of the items is also varied from concrete familiar, to symbolic, to suggestive. It is designed for students in the fourth to twelfth grades. Similar logical principles are examined in both tests. The difference is that in the Class Reasoning test the crucial relationships in the items are between classes of things such as Fords, animals that fly, black things, and cats. Each of these comprises a class or a group, and students are asked to reason using the logical relations among the groups. In the Conditional Reasoning test the content of the items is based upon sentences. These sentences are often in the form,

"If such-and-such is the case, then such-and-such other thing is also the case." The truth of the first sentence is a sufficient condition for the truth of the second.

Here is an example of conditional reasoning using concrete familiar content:

7. Suppose you know that

> If the hat on the table is blue, then it belongs to Joan.
>
> The hat on the table is blue.

Then would this be true?

The hat on the table belongs to Joan.

A. Yes, it must be true.

B. No, it can't be true.

C. Maybe, it may be true or it may not be true.

The keyed answer is **A.**

The reliability of the test was estimated using a test-retest format. Students in grades 5, 7, 9, and 11 were administered the test twice with approximately ten weeks between administrations. Correlations ranged from .65 to .80. Evidence for the validity of the test is similar to that offered for the Class Reasoning test.

Applying our guideline 6 to both the Class Reasoning and Conditional Reasoning tests, we judge that they both cover well the deductive reasoning aspect of critical thinking. In addition, we judge in accord with guideline 3 that the scoring guide is reasonable.

3. Logical Reasoning

This deduction test consists of class reasoning items, often called "syllogisms." It does not test for conditional reasoning, or for reasoning with "or" statements. The test consists of forty items grouped into two equal sections, can be administered in thirty minutes, and is aimed at high school and college students.

Reported reliability estimates for the sections are .80 for college students, .83 for high school students, and for the whole test, .89 and .91 respectively.

The test was developed in the factor analytic tradition, the discussion of which is vague in the manual. The test, according to the authors, tests for a "logical evaluation" factor, which they believe is basically the same as Thurstone's "deduction." Reported correlations with other tests range from .04 (calculus) to .42 (also calculus), but the import of the reported correlations is not clear. Percentile ranks are provided for a high school group (mean age, 16.5 years) and a college group (median age, 21.6 years).

In accord with our first two guidelines, we suggest you examine the directions and items and take the test yourself. Here is one for an example. How would you answer it?

16. No mares are singers.

Some singers are women.

Therefore:

    A.   No women are mares.

    B.   No mares are women.

    C.   Some women are not mares.

    D.   Some singers are not women.

The correct answer, according to the meaning of the term "some" as taught in most deductive logic courses, is **C**. If you chose **D**, you were probably interpreting the word "some" in the second premise as implying, "but not all." This is arguably a correct interpretation, but the ambiguity is a problem that bedevils teachers of beginning deductive logic. Unfortunately, logicians force our everyday way of speaking into special interpretations in order to avoid the ambiguities of everyday speech. The result is that logicians' logic is less useful than we desire for thinking about everyday life issues.

Some deductive logic tests avoid this problem, but most (including the two Cornell deduction tests previously discussed) do not avoid the stilted use of language that you can see in the above example. The deduction sections of more comprehensive critical thinking tests tend to be less stilted.

A special problem with the test lies in its advertising. The catalogue claims that it tests for what is commonly called critical thinking. Because challenging, uncontroversial deduction items are so easy to compose, the temptation to call deduction tests critical thinking tests is strong. We recommend resisting this temptation because people might then be misled. It is important that potential users follow guidelines 1 and 5, recommending a close inspection of the items while asking the question, "Does this cover enough of critical thinking in a balanced manner to be called a comprehensive critical thinking test?" Otherwise, they might be led to believe falsely that the test is a comprehensive measure of critical thinking.

Aside from these problems, the test seems to be an efficient deductive logic test.

4. Test on Appraising Observations

This observation test deals with one of the credibility aspects of critical thinking. It is designed primarily for the senior high school grades, but is also useful for junior high school and college level. Items are cast in the contexts of two stories, the story of a traffic accident in Part A and the story of a group exploring a river in Part B. Each item on the test contains two statements reporting what characters in the stories claim to have observed. The task is to choose which, if either, of the statements is more believable.

Answers are keyed in accord with a set of principles for appraising the believability of statements of observation. There are over thirty-five principles in all, so only representative ones are included in the following list.

An observation statement tends to be believable to the extent that

1. the observer is alert to the situation;

2. the observer has no conflict of interest;

3. the observer is skilled in the technique being used;

4. there is sufficient time for observing;

5. if used, instrumentation is adequate;

6. the statement is made close to the time of observing;

7. the statement is made by the person who did the observing;

8. the statement is not a response to a leading question.

The following examples are taken from the traffic accident story. The first tests the Principle of Observer Alertness, Principle 1 above.

> 1. A policeman is questioning Pierre and Martine. They were in their car at the intersection but were not involved in the accident. Martine is the driver and Pierre, who had been trying to figure out which way to go, is the map reader.
>
> The policeman asks Martine how many cars were at the intersection when the accident occurred. She answers, **"There were three cars."**
>
> Pierre says, "No, **there were five cars."**

Before continuing, decide which, if either, of the two boldface statements you feel you have more reason to believe.

The keyed answer is that Martine's statement is more believable because, being the driver, she would tend to be more alert to the road conditions than someone who was reading a map.

Before you read the commentary on the following item, try to determine which principle from the list the item is testing.

> 3. A policewoman has been asking Mr. Wang and Ms. Vernon questions. She asks Mr. Wang, who was one of the people involved in the accident, whether he had used his signal.

Mr. Wang answers, **"Yes, I did use my signal."**

Ms. Vernon had been driving a car which was not involved in the accident. She tells the officer, **"Mr.Wang did not use his signal.** But this didn't cause the accident."

The principle examined in this item is the one about conflict of interest. Wang is in a conflict of interest because, given that he was involved in the accident, it is in his best interests to have people believe that he used his signal. Otherwise, he could be blamed for the accident. Vernon's statement is, therefore, more believable, all other things being assumed equal.

Note the importance of background beliefs in answering this question. If an examinee is not familiar with the rules about use of turn signals and the danger in not using them, the examinee will not detect the conflict of interest. Thus, we again see the potential for differences in background beliefs leading to differences in scores on a critical thinking test.

Reliability estimates for the test were computed using samples of senior high school students. The estimates range from .58 to .76. Evidence for the validity of the test comes from two sources. First, there is the set of principles, which are comprehensive and which the items on the test cover. Second, effort was taken in the construction of the test to interview students and to retain only those items which tended to require critical thinking to be answered correctly.

Applying guideline 6, we judge that this test adequately covers the credibility of observations. However, it does not cover completely the credibility aspect of critical thinking because there are no items asking students to appraise the credibility of people in authoritative positions.

Chapter Summary

This chapter presents seven guidelines for appraising critical thinking tests, and provides a critical review of available general-knowledge critical thinking tests, both comprehensive and aspect-specific. All but one are multiple-choice tests.

The guidelines are as follows:

1. Pay close attention to the directions, the items, and the scoring guide.
2. Take the test yourself, and compare your answers with those of the scoring guide.
3. Satisfy yourself that the scoring guide is reasonable, but do not expect to agree with it completely for any but deduction items.
4. Ask yourself often, "Does this really test for some aspect of critical thinking?"
5. For purported comprehensive critical thinking tests, ask yourself, "Does this cover enough of critical thinking in a balanced manner to be called a comprehensive critical thinking test?"
6. For purported aspect-specific critical thinking tests, ask yourself, "Does this cover enough of the aspect?"
7. Read the test manual and note the statistical information, but remember that test publishers have a conflict of interest in deciding what information to include and exclude, and remember our warnings about information on reliability.

We have considered eight comprehensive tests of critical thinking. The Watson-Glaser Critical Thinking Appraisal and the Cornell Critical Thinking Tests, Levels X and Z, are the most widely known and used. These three include three central aspects of critical thinking: induction, deduction, and assumption identification. Like all other multiple-choice tests, they neglect critical thinking dispositions. A fifth central aspect, credibility of sources and observations, is included in the Cornell critical thinking tests.

The Ross Test of Higher Cognitive Processes, because it tests for a variety of other things, is less purely a critical thinking test than some others. It attempts to assess students' ability to analyze, synthesize, and evaluate, which are the goals at the upper levels of Bloom's taxonomy. Since critical thinking involves much analysis, synthesis, and evaluation, we have included the test in this review. Although the relation between the sections of the test and the Bloom levels is unclear, the problem probably lies in part with the vagueness of the Bloom's levels.

The New Jersey Test of Reasoning Skills appears to be designed specifically for the Philosophy for Children program. Nevertheless, it tests critical thinking abilities which might be taught outside of that curriculum, so we have included it. It heavily emphasizes deduction.

Judgment: Deductive Logic and Assumption Recognition has, in addition to the sections mentioned in the title, a section on credibility of sources and observations. Its use of the word "valid" will confuse some people, and its neglect of other aspects of critical thinking will disappoint some. Conceived as a criterion-referenced test, it gives no standards for judgment, but, nevertheless, it is a test with potential.

Relatively unknown in North America is Test of Enquiry Skills, which emphasizes the gathering and interpretation of published information and also induction in a science context. It does not test for assumption identification or credibility and only minimally tests for deduction. Of the tests we have described, this one comes closest to being a subject-specific test.

The Ennis-Weir Critical Thinking Essay Test is the only essay test of critical thinking commercially available in either comprehensive or aspect-specific form. It is also the only commercially available test that tests for critical thinking dispositions.

There are four aspect-specific tests of critical thinking. Three of them are deduction tests: the Cornell class and conditional reasoning tests and Logical Reasoning. The other, the Test on Appraising Observations, tests for the ability to judge the credibility of observations.

We have provided a critical review of these commercially available critical thinking tests. With the probable exception of the deduction tests, each contains problems that are endemic to critical thinking testing. In particular, the effects of varying levels of sophistication and varying background beliefs among examinees cannot be completely eliminated. Even the essay test contains these problems, but to a lesser degree because the request for justification calls forth more information about the examinee's actual thinking, thereby revealing differences in background beliefs and levels of sophistication. Unfortunately, even though the deduction tests avoid these problems, they miss many aspects of critical thinking.

Problems not endemic to critical thinking testing but appearing in some tests include testing for an examinee's ideology, incorporating sections that are not critical thinking sections, omitting many aspects of critical thinking, mislabeling sections and whole tests, and using artificial content so that a transfer assumption is required.

Testing for critical thinking dispositions is a challenge that has not yet been fully met. In addition, testing for critical thinking abilities needs considerable work, especially on the endemic problems just mentioned.

Suggested Readings

Arter, J. and Salmon, J. (1987). *Assessing Higher Order Thinking Skills: A Consumer's Guide.* Northwest Regional Educational Laboratory, Evaluation and Assessment, 101 SW Main Street, Suite 500, Portland, OR 97204, 15-31.

Walsh, D. and Paul, R. (1986). *The Goal of Critical Thinking: From Educational Ideal to Educational Reality.* American Federation of Teachers, 555 New Jersey Avenue NW, Washington, DC 20001, 40-44.

Annotated List of Tests Discussed in this Chapter

Cornell Class Reasoning Test, Form X (1964), by Robert H. Ennis, William L. Gardiner, Richard Morrow, Dieter Paulus, and Lucille Ringel. Illinois Critical Thinking Project, University of Illinois, 1310 S. 6th Street, Champaign, IL 61820. Aimed at grades 4-14. Seventy-two items, each containing a premise asserting a class relationship, such as "No A's are B's." Each of twelve logical forms is tested by six items with varying content.

Cornell Conditional Reasoning Test, Form X (1964), by Robert H. Ennis, William Gardiner, John Guzzetta, Richard Morrow, Dieter Paulus, and Lucille Ringel. Illinois Critical Thinking Project, University of Illinois, 1310 S. 6th Street, Champaign, IL 61820. Aimed at grades 4-14. Seventy-two items, each containing as a premise a conditional statement, such as "If a, then b." Each of twelve logical forms is represented by six items with varying content.

Cornell Critical Thinking Test, Level X (1985), by Robert H. Ennis and Jason Millman. Midwest Publications, P.O. Box 448, Pacific Grove, CA 93950. Aimed at grades 4-14. Sections on induction, credibility, observation, deduction, and assumption identification.

Cornell Critical Thinking Test, Level Z (1985), by Robert H. Ennis and Jason Millman. Midwest Publications, P.O. Box 448, Pacific Grove, CA 93950. Aimed at advanced or gifted high school students, college students, and other adults. Sections on induction, credibility, prediction and experimental planning, fallacies (especially equivocation), deduction, definition, and assumption identification.

The Ennis-Weir Critical Thinking Essay Test (1985), by Robert
H. Ennis and Eric Weir. Midwest Publications, P.O. Box
448, Pacific Grove, CA 93950. Aimed at grade 7 through
college. Also intended to be used as a teaching material.
Incorporates getting the point, seeing the reasons and assumptions, stating one's point, offering good reasons,
seeing other possibilities (including other possible
explanations), and responding to and avoiding equivocation, irrelevance, circularity, reversal of an if-then (or other
conditional) relationship, overgeneralization, credibility
problems, and the use of emotive language to persuade.

Judgment: Deductive Logic and Assumption Recognition (1971),
by Edith Shaffer and Joann Steiger. Instructional
Objectives Exchange, P.O. Box 24095, Los Angeles,
CA 90024. Aimed at Grades 7-12. Developed as a
criterion-referenced test, but without specified standards.
Includes sections on deduction, assumption identification,
and credibility, and distinguishes between emotionally
loaded content and other content.

Logical Reasoning (1955), by Alfred F. Hertzka and J.P.
Guilford. Sheridan Psychological Services, Inc., P.O. Box
6101, Orange, CA 92667. Aimed at high school and college students and other adults. Tests for facility with class
reasoning. One premise of each argument includes a
statement asserting a class relationship, such as "No
A's are B's."

New Jersey Test of Reasoning Skills (1983), by Virginia
Shipman. Institute for the Advancement of Philosophy
for Children, Test Division, Montclair State College,
Upper Montclair, NJ 08043. Aimed at grades 4-college.
Sections on the syllogism (which is heavily represented),

assumption identification, induction, good reasons, and kind and degree (which are lightly represented).

Ross Test of Higher Cognitive Processes (1976), by John D. Ross and Catherine M. Ross. Academic Therapy Publications, 20 Commercial Blvd., Novato, CA 94947. Aimed at grades 4-6. Sections on verbal analogies, deduction, assumption identification, word relationships, sentence sequencing, interpreting answers to questions, information sufficiency and relevance in mathematics problems, and analysis of attributes of complex stick figures.

Test on Appraising Observations (1983), by Stephen P. Norris and Ruth King. Aimed at grades 7-14. Institute for Educational Research and Development, Memorial University of Newfoundland, St. John's, Newfoundland, Canada, A1B 3X8. Pairs of statements are compared for their believability. The manual provides principles for judging observation statements which the items serve to test. Two story lines are used.

Test of Enquiry Skills (1979), by Barry J. Fraser. Australian Council for Educational Research Limited, Frederick Street, Hawthorn, Victoria 3122, Australia. Aimed at Australian grades 7-10 (possibly not the suitable grade levels for North America). Sections on using reference materials (library usage, index and table of contents); interpreting and processing information (scales, averages, percentages, proportions, charts and tables, graphs); and critical thinking in science (comprehension of science reading, design of experimental procedures, conclusions and generalizations).

Watson-Glaser Critical Thinking-Appraisal (1980), (2 forms), by
Goodwin Watson and Edward M. Glaser. The
Psychological Corporation, 555 Academic Court, San
Antonio, TX 78204. Aimed at grade 9 through adulthood.
Sections on induction, assumption identification, deduc-
tion, judging whether conclusions logically follow beyond
a reasonable doubt, and argument evaluation.

CHAPTER FOUR

MAKING YOUR OWN MULTIPLE-CHOICE CRITICAL THINKING TESTS

Suppose that the commercially available critical thinking tests are not adequate for your purposes, and you set out to make your own. How should you go about it?

In this chapter we shall offer practical advice on making some standard kinds of multiple-choice items and tests. In chapter 5 we focus on more open-ended approaches: essay and short-answer testing, interviewing, and monitoring classroom discussions. Our general approach in both chapters emphasizes students' understanding and the meaning of the information, rather than statistical analyses, although we believe that at least simple statistical information is always helpful.

The following topics are the principal ones of this chapter:

(1) identifying the purpose of the test,

(2) making a table of specifications, and

(3) drafting items that satisfy the table of specifications.

Under this last topic we shall offer some background considerations, general item-writing advice, and some specific advice for items in the areas of deduction, credibility, induction, and assumption identification.

Section One: Identifying the Purpose of the Test

What is to be the purpose of the test? Although it is tempting to say, "Of course the purpose is to test critical thinking," this is not enough. Identification of a more specific purpose is necessary for making a number of decisions. We thus begin this chapter about constructing your own multiple-choice critical thinking tests with a brief discussion of various purposes you might have in mind. We will return to discuss the purposes of critical-thinking evaluation in chapter 6.

> > *Testing for transfer*

As the authors of volume 1 pointed out, one important justification for teaching critical thinking is that it will help students think critically about matters other than those found in school subjects. Since it is dangerous to assume that transfer will occur automatically from thinking about school subjects to other activities of life, one purpose might be to test whether transfer has taken place. Having this purpose should incline us to use other than subject-specific content and to use forms of testing that more closely approximate situations that arise outside of school subjects, such as responding to a letter to the editor, or discussing an issue with another student or with a group of students.

> > *Testing for critical thinking in specific subjects*

If testing for transfer is not the purpose, but we want to see whether students have learned to think in a particular subject, then it is probably best to use content from that area in the testing. There is much room for the development of critical thinking tests that use content from specific subjects.

> > *Preparing students for multiple-choice testing*

Although multiple-choice testing is not always the best approach to evaluation, its economic advantages make it a prevalent form of testing. Thus, teachers often feel the need to prepare students to take standardized multiple-choice tests, even though their educational instincts are not to prepare students explicitly for certain types of tests. If this is the purpose, then the multiple-choice form is probably the best to use.

>> *Judging students vs. judging programs*

If we want to appraise individual students, then the test must be much more reliable and valid for each individual student than if we want to appraise programs. In appraising programs, mistakes about individual students tend to cancel out and get lost in the averages. But for an individual student, a quirk of invalidity can be seriously unfair.

So a test used to judge individual students must be much more finely honed. One way to attempt this is to provide a large number of items. Another way is to make the inference from students' responses to the judgment about their critical thinking more dependable, perhaps by requesting justification for answers to multiple-choice items. We shall have more to say about this strategy for modifying multiple-choice tests.

>> *Summative vs. formative evaluation*

Formative evaluations are carried out when the development of a course or program is in progress. Through formative evaluations we seek ideas for improvements that might be made in the program or teaching methodology. Summative evaluations, on the other hand, are conducted after a program or course has been developed. Here, judgments are made about whether or not the program or teaching method works, reaches its goals, or reaches its goals better than the alternatives. Information gathered as a program proceeds is less likely to be subject to public scrutiny and less likely to have broad final consequences than information that is gathered at the end to evaluate the success of the program. Because of this, formative evaluations need not be so finely honed as summative evaluations.

>> *Aspect-specific vs. comprehensive testing*

If we want to diagnose students' weaknesses and strengths in particular aspects of critical thinking, then we need scores on each of these aspects. If the aspects are tested by separate sections in comprehensive tests, then the sections should be treated as separate aspect-specific tests with appropriate attention given to their individual reliabilities and validities. For a comprehensive appraisal, less fine honing is required for each section.

>> *Norm-referenced testing vs. criterion-referenced testing*

In norm-referenced testing, students' scores are interpreted by determining where they fall compared to those of other students. If we want to compare students with each other in this way, then it is often considered wise to try to make items that are answered correctly by between 25% and 75% of the students. This spreads out students' scores over a greater range, making comparison easier.

In the testing field, incidentally, this recommendation is stated by saying that we should try to get items that are between the .25 and .75 *difficulty levels.* But note that in the testing field the proportion of students who get an item *right* is referred to as the item's "difficulty." Care must be taken in using this term because its technical meaning is not the same as its everyday meaning. First, a high number indicates an item that is *not* difficult in this technical sense. Second, in the everyday sense, an item may be more difficult than another even though more students get the more difficult item right. This can happen if, for instance, the students rise to the challenge of the more difficult item, but work carelessly with the easier item. In the technical sense of difficulty, the everyday-sense-more-difficult item might be the easier one. The technical sense can therefore be confusing.

In criterion-referenced testing, students are not compared to each other but to a satisfactory standard of performance which has been set in advance. This comparison process allows us to say what proportion of a given area of knowledge students know compared to how much would be deemed satisfactory. Thus, items need to be constructed so that they adequately cover the area of knowledge in question.

>> *Testing for grading*

There are at least two possible purposes behind spreading out scores—norm-referencing as described above and grading. Sometimes teachers attempt to spread out scores to make it easier to justify differences in grades. Sometimes the goal is that a certain percentage of students receive a certain grade; for example, that only 20% receive an "A." Although this latter purpose has some practical justification, we do not endorse it.

Section Two: Making a Table of Specifications

Given that you have decided on the test purpose, you must then decide what sorts of things to put in the test. What aspects of critical thinking do you want to include? If the test is to be subject-specific, what elements of the subject do you want to include? How do you want to weight these aspects and elements?

A *table of specifications* is a good way to represent your answers to these questions. Table 4.1 is a simple example of such a table for a general knowledge critical thinking test. It gives equal weights of 25% to each of four aspects of critical thinking, indicating that one-fourth of the items will be devoted to each aspect.

Suppose that we want to test for critical thinking in the field of economics, using the same four aspects, but also allocating items among the following five major areas of economics: money, economic growth, inflation, taxes, and international trade. Then a *two-way* table of specifications similar to the one in table 4.2 would be appropriate.

Table 4.2 preserves the critical thinking weighting of table 4.1—25% for each of the four aspects—and as well allocates equally each of the four aspects to each of the five areas of economics. Each cell in table 4.2 represents the percentage weighting given to the combination of the given area of economics with the given aspect of critical thinking. For example, the upper left-hand cell represents a weighting of 5% for the combination of money and deduction, that is, 5% of the items should test for deducing in the area of money. Since we assumed equal weighting for each area and aspect, each combination is weighted 5% out of the total

Table 4.1. Table of Specifications for a
General Knowledge Multiple-Choice
Critical Thinking Test

Aspect	*Weighting*
Deduction	25%
Credibility of Sources and Observations	25%
Induction	25%
Unstated-Assumption Identification	25%
Total	100%

of 100%. If there were to be 100 items on the test, then there would be five items for each cell in the table of specifications.

Actually, all of this is idealized. Items usually are not pure tests of only one area of a subject or one aspect of critical thinking, since areas of subjects and aspects of critical thinking are interdependent. So one must make judgments, based on what one thinks to be the predominant emphasis of an item, so that the table of specifications is roughly satisfied.

Section Three: Drafting Items

In this section we shall present (1) some preliminary considerations, (2) some general rules for item writing, and (3) a detailed look at writing items for the four aspects of critical thinking in tables 4.1 and 4.2. In order for the examples to be understood by all readers, we shall not use subject-specific items. Note that a significant omission from the aspects of critical thinking listed in the tables is critical thinking dispositions. Dispositions are left out

Table 4.2. Specifications for a Subject-Specific
Multiple-Choice Critical Thinking Test
in Economics

Aspects of Critical Thinking

Area of Economics	Deduction	Credibility	Induction	Assumption Identification	Row Totals
Money	5%	5%	5%	5%	20%
Economic Growth	5%	5%	5%	5%	20%
Inflation	5%	5%	5%	5%	20%
Taxes	5%	5%	5%	5%	20%
International Trade	5%	5%	5%	5%	20%
Column Totals	25%	25%	25%	25%	100%

because we do not see a way to test for them using multiple-choice tests.

>> *Preliminary considerations*

Being well versed. It is important for item writers to be well versed in critical thinking and in the content, either general knowledge or subject-specific, which the test is designed to test. Many mistakes are made because this consideration is ignored.

Elements of an item. Basic elements of an item are (1) the test directions, (2) the context in which the task is set, (3) the item stem, (4) the choices, and (5) the scoring key. All are essential, and no thinking about an item is complete unless all of these elements are considered.

Close attention to the meaning of an item. Throughout the coming discussion, you will note our attention to meaning. We urge you to be sensitive to the meanings of the words and sentences you use and to the interpretations that students might place upon them. If students misunderstand your request, then the test itself will fail—not the students. To minimize this problem, we suggest that you try your items on yourself and continually ask, "Is the meaning clear?"

>> *General rules for item writing*

Here are some general rules for item writing, based upon a set prepared by Jason Millman of Cornell University. Like all general rules, they have exceptions. However, they are useful guidelines, and we shall assume them in our detailed discussion of writing items for specific aspects of critical thinking.

1. Construct each item with one and only one correct or best answer.

2. Test for the intended knowledge and abilities by:

   a. avoiding trivial questions and including questions about important facts and concepts, and

   b. including questions emphasizing higher level thinking ability rather than rote recall.

3. Avoid "none of the above" and "all of the above" as choices when examinees are to choose the best, rather than the precisely correct, answer.

4. Use either a direct question or an incomplete statement as the item stem.

5. Write items in clear and simple language.

6. State the central problem of the item clearly and completely in the stem.

7. Include most of the reading in the stem.

8. Base each item on a single, central problem.

9. Construct options homogeneous in grammatical form.

10. Include in the stem any words that would otherwise need repeating in each option.

11. Emphasize negative words or words of exclusion (e.g., "not," "except") and avoid such words when possible.

12. Place options at the *end* of the item stem, not in the middle of it.

13. Arrange the options in a logical order, if one exists.

14. Make all options plausible to examinees who do not know the correct or best answer.

15. Avoid unintended hints based on:

    a. grammatical consistency or inconsistency between the stem and the option,

    b. repetition of key words in the stem and keyed option, or

    c. rote or other verbal associations between key words in the stem and the keyed option.

16. Avoid hints based on the:

    a. unusual length of the keyed option,

    b. degree of qualification stated in the keyed option or use of terms such as "never" and "always" in the unkeyed options,

    c. lack of independence and mutual exclusivity of the options,

    d. frequency with which the keyed option is placed in a given option position, or

    e. pattern of the location of the keyed position.

17. Avoid hints from one item to another.

>> Writing Items for the Four Aspects Of Critical Thinking

In the following pages we will look in detail at item writing for the four aspects of critical thinking we have listed in tables 4.1 and 4.2.

Deduction items. Since deduction items are the easiest items to write, we will begin with them. The basic question in deduction is always whether a statement necessarily follows from one or more other statements.

The comparative-judgment approach. In the comparative-judgment approach to multiple-choice deduction items, the examinee is given several statements and asked to choose which one of several others follows. Examinees are told implicitly or explicitly that at least one follows, and they only have to choose from among the possibilities. We call this approach the comparative-judgment approach because examinees must choose the *best* of those given, *compared* to the rest. Here is an example from the Cornell Level X test:

> 53.   "If these beings are from Earth, then another space ship must have landed on Nicoma. But no other space ship has landed on Nicoma."
>
> Which follows?
>
> A.   Another space ship has landed on Nicoma.
>
> B.   These beings are not from Earth.
>
> C.   These beings came here by mistake.

The noncomparative-judgment approach. In the noncomparative-judgment approach, examinees are asked to judge whether or not a given conclusion follows. The judgment is noncomparative because candidates are to judge about one particular thing whether or not *it* follows necessarily. Either it does or it does not, and they are asked to decide. Here is an example that is a revision of Item 53 and is modeled after the form used in the Cornell deduction tests:

53R. "If these beings are from Earth, then another space ship must have landed on Nicoma. But no other space ship has landed on Nicoma."

Suppose that what the speaker says is true. Then must this be true?

These beings are not from Earth.

A. Yes, it must be true.

B. No, it cannot be true.

C. We cannot tell for sure from the information given.

The correct answer, "Yes, it must be true," does not depend on comparing the possible conclusion with some others. So it is a noncomparative-judgment item.

Item 53R adds another wrinkle. It offers the alternative, "No, it cannot be true," which would be an appropriate response to conclusions that actually contradict the given information. One reason for this additional alternative is to make wild guessing less successful. Another is to give students a chance to show that they can see contradictions, a basic skill in deduction.

The principal advantage of the noncomparative-judgment approach to deduction items is that it shows whether examinees see the standard logical fallacies, that is, whether they see that certain standard moves in logic are invalid. The comparative-judgment approach does not give us this assurance. But the comparative-judgment approach, all other things equal, gives a logically easier task.

Summary and comment. To draft a deduction item,

(1) provide some information that examinees are to assume to be true; and

(2) either provide several possible conclusions and ask which one follows (the comparative-judgment approach), or provide just one possible conclusion and ask whether it follows (the noncomparative-judgment approach).

A variation on the noncomparative-judgment approach adds the alternative that the proposition in question contradicts the original material. Many other variations are possible.

Deduction items are popular. One reason for this is that nontrivial deduction items with clearly correct answers are easier to make than items for other aspects of critical thinking. For example, there is no doubt that **B** is the correct answer to Item 53 above, but there are many examinees who do not see that this answer is correct.

Another reason for their popularity is the importance of deduction as an integral part of other aspects of critical thinking. Although not many arguments in our everyday lives are totally deductive in nature, deduction plays a role in many aspects of critical thinking, such as definition, assumption identification, and predicting from hypotheses.

Self-test. It would be helpful now for you to stop reading and to make a few deduction items yourself, review them, secure others' opinions about them, give them to some examinees like your target examinees, and interview these examinees to see why they answered the way they did. In order not to be threatening, tell the examinees that you are not testing them but rather are testing your test items.

Credibility items. The basis of credibility judgment is the use of general principles that say what tends to increase the believability of what people say. Of the four types of critical thinking items in our table of specifications, credibility items are the second easiest to make. They are more difficult to make than deduction items because of the dependence of credibility judgments on background beliefs about how the physical, social, and cultural worlds work.

Comparative judgment. Since judgments of credibility must rely on context and we really cannot judge out of context whether to believe a particular person, credibility items should request comparative judgments. Here is an item from the Cornell Level X which calls for a comparative judgment:

27. A.   The health officer says, <u>"This water is safe to drink."</u>

   B.   Several others are soldiers. One of them says, <u>"This water supply is not safe."</u>

   C.   <u>A</u> and <u>B</u> are equally believable.

Examinees are asked to judge which, if either, underlined statement is more believable.

The general formula exhibited by Item 27, lodged as it is in the context of exploring the planet Nicoma, is shown in table 4.3.

Noncomparative judgments. A noncomparative-judgment item might look like this:

27R.   The health officer says, <u>"This water is safe to drink."</u>

   Should you believe the health officer?

   A.   Yes.

   B.   No.

   C.   Cannot tell.

The correct answer to 27R is **C**. In fact, if credibility items were presented as noncomparative-judgment items, then the proper answer to every item (except those quoting an infallible authority) is "Cannot tell." Not enough information can be presented in a test item for a noncomparative judgment on credibility. So the noncomparative-judgment approach is not satisfactory for credibility items.

Background beliefs. As we pointed out in chapter 3, it is unfair to penalize examinees for having different background beliefs than those of the test-maker, unless of course the background beliefs are part of the subject matter that the examinees are to have mastered.

So the item-writer must deal with the background belief problem when making credibility items. One way to reduce the problem is to provide considerable context for items, thus eliminating some deviant beliefs. Another is to interview representative examinees

114 EVALUATING CRITICAL THINKING

Table 4.3. General Formula for a Credibility
Comparative-Judgment Item

1. Provide a context.

2. Provide two clearly identified conflicting state-
    ments, using underlining or some other device to
    indicate the exact statements in question.

3. Provide a basis for making a credibility judgment,
    but make sure that the statements are otherwise
    equally plausible.

4. Ask which, if either, is more credible.

---

about prospective items, asking them to say why they chose their answers. If variation in significant background beliefs is found, then items can be modified or eliminated. A third way is to think about some prospective examinees (your own students, for example) and to make educated guesses about possible variations in their background beliefs.

Multiple-choice justification of original answer. A fourth way to deal with differences in background beliefs that is not now implemented in commercial tests is to ask a second multiple-choice item about the examinee's answer to the first one. This second item might offer several possible justifications for answers to the first item. Scoring would then be of a pair of responses. One answer to the first item with a suitable choice of justification in the second item might be just as good as a different first answer with another justification. However, it is difficult to write the second item in such a way that there are wrong answers to the pairs that are attractive enough to be selected.

A justification item to pair with the Cornell Level X Item 27 might go as follows:

28R. A good reason for your answer to Item 27 is:

    A. Soldiers are likely to know more about the safety of water supplies than health officers.

    B. Health officers are likely to know more about the safety of water supplies than soldiers.

    C. The health officer did not test the water.

Answer **B** on 27 paired with **A** on 28R, and **A** on 27 paired with **B** on 28R would each receive full credit. Any other combination would be wrong. In particular, **C** on 28R would be wrong because no such information was ever given.

The pair of items, 27 and 28R, would then take care of the examinee who believes that soldiers are more likely to be experts about water supplies than health officers. If such a person also believes that expertise counts in favor of credibility, which is what the original item is trying to test, the person would receive full credit for the answer.

However, there are difficulties. One is that the justification choices might suggest things to examinees, such as expertise about the safety of water supplies, that otherwise would not have occurred to them. If it is made impossible for examinees to change answers to the first item after seeing the choice of justifications, the difficulty of writing a good second item is lessened. This approach is possible with tests presented on a computer.

Another difficulty is that we cannot in advance state all the reasonable justifications that examinees might have. A third difficulty is that psychometric theory generally assumes items that are independent of each other. These are not overwhelming difficulties, but they do give cause for concern.

Open-ended request for justification. A fifth way to take into account variations in background beliefs is to add an open-ended request for the examinee to defend the answer to the original item. This would eliminate machine scorability and thus raise costs. But it would leave open the possibility of giving credit to someone who is thinking well but had some reason that is not included in the ones supplied by the test maker. It would also avoid the problem of suggesting reasons to examinees that they might not have had when answering the original item.

Self-test. It is now time for you to write a few credibility items. You will find that it is more difficult than it seems. First, check the criteria for credibility of sources and observations given in the appendix. Then draft a few items that test for some of the criteria. After you have done this, show your items to a colleague to see how he or she would answer them. Then revise the items, give them to a few students, and solicit their thinking by asking them why they answered as they did. Then revise the items again and give them to a class, soliciting the students' reactions and justifications for their answers. After these experiences and their accompanying surprises, you will be better able to draft credibility items for your various purposes.

Induction items. Induction items deal with situations in which conclusions do not necessarily follow from the evidence, since there are other explanations or conclusions possible. There are two types of induction: (1) generalizing, in which the conclusion is simply a generalization of the evidence; and (2) inference to best explanation, in which the conclusion gets its strength from its ability to explain the facts better than all plausible alternatives. The background-belief problem and the level-of-sophistication problem are always present in induction testing, and we shall discuss strategies to circumvent them.

The problems are exemplified by the Watson-Glaser item about Mr. Brown's keeping his pool hall open after 1 a.m., discussed in chapter 3 (p. 58). The choices there were "True," "Probably True," "Insufficient Data," "Probably False," and "False." The level-of-sophistication problem was apparent in that item, since different powers to imagine how pool halls operate and how people relate to each other could justify an answer of "Insufficient Data," instead of the keyed answer, "Probably True." Furthermore, an answer of "True" would be justified for a student who had been taught in civics class that people regularly incur fines of that magnitude only if it is to their interest—a background-belief problem.

Degree of discrimination. It might help to request less fine discrimination than that requested on the Watson-Glaser test. For example, we might ask students to tell only whether the evidence supports the conclusion, goes against the conclusion, or neither. Roughly speaking, this approach puts "True" and "Probably True" under "Supports"; "False" and "Probably False" under "Goes Against"; and "Insufficient Data" under "Neither." Then the person who could think of a number of other explanations might still choose "Supports" because that involves considerably less commitment than "Probably True." The student who believes that people incur fines only if it is in their interest could also justifiably choose "Supports."

The general directions for the induction section might then look like this:

For each conclusion decide whether the given information (A) supports it, (B) goes against it, or (C) neither.

These directions are probably better than asking for a five-choice discrimination among "True," "Probably True," "Insufficient Data," "Probably False," and "False." But they do not solve all background-belief and level-of-sophistication problems, as we have discovered with the Cornell critical thinking tests, which use a three-fold choice like that suggested.

Interviewing others. It always helps to interview colleagues and students about prospective items in order to get an idea of what interpretations and background beliefs might be employed by examinees. Items can accordingly be refined or abandoned.

Providing extensive background information. Another possibility is to provide a wealth of background information in the test itself. Information to include might be suggested in the interviews mentioned in the previous paragraph. But this can make a time-consuming reading load for examinees.

Alternatively, the test could use content in a subject area familiar to students, thus reducing differences in background beliefs. The reading load problem is also thereby reduced or avoided.

No perfect solution. But there is no perfect solution, especially if we adhere to straight multiple-choice testing. You can rest assured that some good critical thinkers will differ with the key. So do not expect perfect scores. If it is a criterion-referenced test, do not set your criterion at 100%. Perhaps you might set the criterion at 80% or 90% correct in order for people to be judged thoroughly competent at the level of sophistication you are testing.

All this assumes a test based on general knowledge. For a subject-specific test, in which you can insist on certain background beliefs, you might set the criterion higher. But still do not expect complete agreement among good critical thinkers in a subject. Remember that leading figures in various fields of study disagree about what may be concluded from available information.

Asking for justification. A better approach to induction testing is to ask examinees to write reasons for their answers. This introduces the need for a human scorer and is thus more costly, but it will be more likely to reveal background beliefs for which students should not be penalized. If you are using a subject-specific test, then the procedure will also help reveal mistaken background beliefs for which they should be penalized.

There is another possibility in between asking for a written justification and asking only for the standard multiple-choice judgment: offering another multiple-choice item presenting possible justifications. Then, as with the similar suggestion for credibility items, the items could be paired. This is a suggestion that has not been explored thoroughly for induction items, and it appears at first glance difficult to implement. Perhaps such an item following item 6 of the Watson-Glaser Mr. Brown example could look like this:

7R.   What was your reason for answering Item 6 as you did?

A. The answer I picked offered the most plausible explanation of the information provided.

B. There are many other possible and plausible explanations of the information provided.

C. It could not have been to Mr. Brown's advantage to keep his pool hall open on some nights. Six fines of $500 are too expensive.

Summary. Induction items are concerned with conclusions that do not necessarily follow from the evidence or reasons that support them. Examinees' background beliefs and levels of sophistication justifiably influence their answers. The problem resulting from this influence can be reduced by:

(1)   providing much background information in one of a variety of ways,

(2)   by asking for a justification of the examinees' answers, and

(3)   by interviewing colleagues and students in order to identify prospective troubling beliefs and perspectives.

Since there always will be a shortage of information provided with the test item, distinctions between alternatives should probably be quite broad, such as the three-way distinction: (1) supports, (2) goes against, and (3) neither.

Self-test. It is time for you to try to write some induction items yourself. Following the advice given in the summary that you have just read, compose two or three induction items and try them out with colleagues and students, as you did with your deduction and credibility items.

Assumption-identification items. The word "assumption" has at least three different threads of meaning in our language. Thus students can interpret a request to identify an assumption in one way when you mean it in another. So you need to be familiar with the alternatives if you are to write good assumption-identification items. The topic is difficult and complicated. Therefore, you might have to read the following discussion several times and think about it for awhile before you can make use of it.

In one sense, an assumption is a *tentatively held conclusion,* as in the statement, "I assume that you are going out, since you are wearing your hat." The assumption in this case is "You are going out," and it is a tentatively held conclusion.

In another sense, calling something an assumption has a *pejorative force.* That is, to call something an assumption is frequently to demean it, as in "That's just an assumption."

In a third sense, an assumption is *part of the basis of someone's reasoning* about what to believe or do. Suppose someone said, "The speaker is probably assuming that only males have short hair," after the speaker said, "Since about half of the villagers have very short hair, I think that at least half are male." Then the person would be pointing out a basis of the speaker's reasoning which the speaker left implicit.

This third sense of assumption is what people generally mean when they specify *identifying implicit assumptions* as a critical thinking goal, and is what we mean by it in this book.

A Danger in an Open-ended Request. If you just ask your students in an open-ended request to list the assumptions in a passage, you will get an array that mixes all three senses together. In particular, you will get a heavy dosage of conclusions that are thought to be dubious by the students. Thus, you might not be testing their ability to identify implicit assumptions in the sense in which this goal is usually stated.

Inadvertently asking for conclusions. If you make an assumption-identification item without being clear about these threads of meaning, students might draw a tentative conclusion from the information given, instead of identifying implicit assumptions in it. From materials distributed in California, here is an example that was claimed to test for the ability to identify implicit assumptions:

The following figures from the U.S. Bureau of the Census show the percent of eligible voters who cast ballots in national elections.

1968	1972	1976	1980
60.9%	55.2%	53.5%	52.6%

From these figures it can be assumed that

A.   voters are becoming more dissatisfied with available candidates.

B.   a majority of Americans don't vote.

C.   voter turnout has been steadily declining for more than a decade.

D.   voter participation has reached an all-time low.

This looks like a good item, but it does not test for ability to identify implicit assumptions, even though it uses the word "assumed." Instead, it tests for ability to draw a tentative conclusion from data. To make this slip is to lower the weighting assigned to the important goal of identifying implicit assumptions. (Incidentally, when the item finally appeared on the Eighth Grade History-Social Science Test of the California Assessment Program, it had been revised and the word "assumed" was replaced by the word "concluded.")

Avoiding the confusion. One way to avoid the confusion between conclusions and implicit assumptions is to avoid having conclusions among the options. If there are no conclusions in the set of options, then conclusions cannot be picked, and we avoid penalizing a person for interpreting the word "assume" in a different way from the intended sense.

Comparative vs. noncomparative approaches. As with the other types of critical thinking items, there are comparative and noncomparative ways of asking for assumption identification. An example of the comparative approach is, "Which is most probably assumed?" followed by several choices. An example of the noncomparative approach is to ask about a particular possible assumption, "Was this assumed?" Since ingenious people usually have difficulty saying for certain that something was assumed, we recommend the comparative approach. Consider this example from the Watson-Glaser test:

> "I'm traveling to South America. I want to be sure that I do not get typhoid fever, so I shall go to my physician and get vaccinated against typhoid fever before I begin my trip."
>
> Proposed assumption:
>
> 28. Typhoid fever is more common in South America than it is where I live.
>
> MADE or NOT MADE?

The key claims that the assumption is MADE. It is true that the proposed assumption would provide a basis for going to the physician. However, a basis could readily be constructed that denies the proposed assumption. Suppose, for example, that the reasoner holds that typhoid fever is *less* common in South America, but that the consequences are more serious if contracted there. That, too, would provide a basis for going to the physician, but it contradicts the proposition keyed as MADE. Since ingenious people can usually find a way around pinning one particular assumption on a position, it is better not to ask for a noncomparative judgment. It is better to ask for a comparative judgment, such as "Which (of several statements) is probably taken for granted?"

Asking for necessary assumptions. Although it is tempting to think that certain assumptions are logically necessary for an argument or position, they are not. So do not ask for them. Consider this item from the Cornell Level X test, and try to decide what is the keyed answer:

> 70. "Since about half of the villagers have very short hair, I think that at least half are male." Which is probably taken for granted?

   A. Half are female.

   B. All males have short hair.

   C. Only males have short hair.

The keyed answer is **C**. The addition of **C** to the reason given ("Half of the villagers have very short hair") yields the conclusion that the speaker wants to draw ("At least half are male"). So **C** serves as an adequate basis for the inference that the speaker draws, but neither of the others does.

Suppose, however, that we had asked "Which is *necessarily* taken for granted?" instead of, "Which is *probably* taken for granted?" Then if the examinee interprets the word "necessarily" to indicate logical necessity, as many do, then no answer is correct. The argument does not necessarily depend on **C**. Note that **C** is a very broad generalization. The argument could go through with a much weaker basis, such as "In this tribe only the males have short hair" or "On the planet Nicoma only males have short hair." A good critical thinker might still get the item right, even with the word "necessarily" included in the question, because **C** is better than the others. But the word "necessarily" in the direction would at least slow down some good critical thinkers and force them to waste time. It might also force them to omit the item or guess wildly.

Unfortunately, two nationally available published tests ask for necessary assumptions. The New Jersey test asks "What *must* [name] assume?" The Watson-Glaser test interprets "Not Made" as meaning "Not Necessarily Made." The error is more serious in the Watson-Glaser test, because it asks for noncomparative judgments. Since no significant assumptions are logically necessarily made, "Not made" sometimes becomes the right answer in this test, even when the key claims that "Made" is the right answer. The discriminating critical thinker thereby is penalized for using good critical thinking.

Writing assumption-identification items. In table 4.4 there is a set of guidelines for writing multiple-choice assumption-identification items based upon the previous discussion.

If you wish to use constructed-response items, then asking for an open-ended justification for assumption-identification items can be very helpful and would have saved the typhoid item above because it would reveal how examinees think about the item. The value of multiple-choice justification, however, seems doubtful. On the basis of those that we have tried, we feel that the provision of justifications gives away the answers to assumption-identification items. But the idea might be further explored.

Table 4.4. Guidelines for Writing
Assumption-identification Items

1. Provide a context consisting of an argument or an explanation with some of its basis not included;

2. Provide three or more options for this missing basis.

3. Make sure that none of these options is a conclusion that can be drawn from the information.

4. Make sure that one and only one fills the gap in the explanation or argument.

5. Ask which is probably taken for granted or assumed.

A note on presuppositions. Another kind of implicit assumption is the *presupposition.* It does not provide a basis for an argument or explanation, but it is something that must be true if some concept or statement is to be meaningfully applied. For example, suppose someone asks, "Has he stopped cheating at cards?" This question *presupposes* that he used to cheat at cards. If he did not, then the question cannot meaningfully be directly answered. An answer of "Yes" and an answer of "No" would both imply acceptance of the presupposition. Since we are sometimes fooled into accepting poorly supported presuppositions, it is good to be alert for them.

Very little of the advice we gave for implicit assumptions that provide a basis for arguments or explanations seems to fit the identification of presuppositions. Generally, it seems difficult to frame significant multiple-choice questions that test for ability to identify presuppositions because they are so obvious if they are picked out for us. Imagine the following item:

"Has he stopped cheating at cards?"

Proposed assumption:

He used to cheat at cards.

MADE or NOT MADE?

Of course the assumption is made. But that follows simply from our knowing the meaning of words and the usual content of their utterance, once someone else points out the presupposition, as must be done in multiple-choice items. The important ability in identifying presuppositions is being able to notice in a real context significant presuppositions that are embedded in some statements and questions, and being ready to wonder about these things if appropriate. This could be tested in an open-ended situation, but the multiple-choice situation seems inappropriate since the item itself does the significant work of calling attention to the presupposition.

Summary. We have noted three different threads in the meaning of the word "assumption": the conclusion thread, the pejorative thread, and the basis thread. Because of these independent meanings, it is easy to confuse examinees, and it is easy for item writers themselves to be confused if they are not familiar with distinguishing between these threads of meaning.

Identifying implicit assumptions refers to basis-type assumptions. These provide part of the backing or basis for a decision. If the assumption is false, then the decision it backs is discredited. That provides the motivation for identifying implicit assumptions.

In writing assumption-identification items for explanation and argument contexts,

- provide a context that includes an argument or explanation;
- provide several alternative possible assumptions, no one of which is a conclusion;
- make sure that one and only one option fills the gap in the argument or explanation;
- ask which is probably taken for granted; and
- do not suggest that the assumption is necessary.

Most of this advice does not hold for presuppositions, which must be true if a question or statement can be meaningfully applied in the situation. But testing for the ability to identify presuppositions seems pointless in a multiple-choice test. Once the presupposition is pointed out, the important work is done.

Self-test. It is time for you to try to write some assumption-identification items yourself. Following the advice given in the summary that you have just read, compose two or three items and try them out with colleagues and students, as you did with your deduction, credibility, and induction items.

Chapter Summary

Making items for multiple-choice tests was the primary concern of this chapter. We demonstrated the importance of making one's purpose explicit; exhibited the use of a table of specifications; presented some general rules for writing multiple-choice items; and gave some specific advice for constructing items in the critical thinking areas of deduction, credibility, induction, and identifying implicit assumptions.

A major problem for all but possibly the deduction items is the differences in background beliefs and levels of sophistication of examinees. They may be thinking well, but choosing answers that are keyed wrong. Suggestions for minimizing this and other problems are given in table 4.5 on the next page.

There is much more to be said about these topics, and many refinements could be made. We hope that the basic ideas we have presented will be helpful to you in making items from the four areas selected for exemplification, and will stimulate you to develop similar ideas for other aspects of critical thinking. We hope that our basic rule—*pay close attention to the meaning*—in combination with the specific advice we have given, will equip you to make items for your own situation.

Table 4.5. Suggestions for Minimizing Problems
in Item Writing

1. Use the comparative-judgment approach for credi-
    bility, induction, and assumption-identification items.

2. Use the noncomparative-judgment approach for
    deduction items.

3. Provide as much context as is permitted by the
    reading load.

4. Interview examinees who are like the target exami-
    nees in order to see what sorts of background
    beliefs and levels of sophistication they bring to
    the items.

5. Add an item that offers possible justifications for the
    options in the original item, but be aware that you
    might be giving examinees ideas they would not
    otherwise have.

6. Add an open-ended request to examinees to explain
    why they answered as they did.

7. Be well informed about critical thinking and the topic
    of the item, whether it be general knowledge or some
    specific school subject.

8. Beware of the different threads of meaning associ-
    ated with the term, "assumption": conclusions, pe-
    jorative force, and basis. Arrange things so that you
    are really testing for the *basis* type of assumptions.

CHAPTER FIVE

MAKING YOUR OWN OPEN-ENDED INFORMATION-GATHERING TECHNIQUES

In chapters 3 and 4, we illustrated some of the strengths and weaknesses of multiple-choice critical thinking tests. This form of testing should not be dismissed lightly, as it can serve many important roles in critical thinking evaluation. However, a complete evaluation of critical thinking requires more than multiple-choice testing as a source of information.

Short-answer critical thinking testing, requesting argumentative essays, interviewing individual students as they work on problems, and carefully monitoring the discussions in a classroom are also useful information-gathering techniques. As we indicated in a general way in chapter 2, these more open-ended approaches have several advantages over multiple-choice critical thinking testing. First, they provide the evaluator more opportunity to take into account the effects of different background beliefs and levels of sophistication among students. Second, they provide clearer insight into critical thinking dispositions. Third, their ecological validity is greater; that is, they give a better indication of critical thinking in important tasks that seem less concocted than multiple-choice test situations. One must not forget, however, that each of these approaches exacts a greater toll in time and money than multiple-choice testing.

In this chapter we will provide guidelines and examples for using these open-ended approaches. Their open-endedness makes it difficult to provide guidance as clear as that given for multiple-choice testing. However, we will be as specific as we can.

To begin, we will list some general guidelines which apply to all open-ended approaches. Then, we will examine an example of short-answer testing in the area of reading, show how the general guidelines apply, and suggest some additional guides which are specific to this format. The use of argumentative essays, that is, essays which present and defend a thesis, is the next topic. We will offer some guidelines for assigning such essays and for grading them. After this, we will illustrate an interview approach, using the context of a fictitious traffic accident, and again offer some guidelines specific to that approach. Finally, we will offer some advice on gathering information on students' critical thinking by monitoring classroom discussions (using an example from American history) and again provide some specific guidelines for that approach.

General Guidelines for Open-ended Approaches

The discussion in the first and second sections of chapter 4 concerning the purposes and content emphasis of multiple-choice testing applies as well to open-ended approaches. Therefore, you might wish to review those sections now, making alterations to the discussion as needed. For example, the general notion of a table of specifications can apply to open-ended approaches, but weightings will probably need to be more vague because open-ended approaches cannot be conveniently divided into items.

The general advice offered in chapter 4 that you be well informed, both about critical thinking and the topic of the evaluation, also applies to open-ended evaluation. Indeed, because of the degree of interpretation required to understand students' short paragraphs and essays, their responses to interview questions, and their discussions in class, the need to be well informed is even greater when using open-ended approaches.

In table 5.1 are some general guidelines (additional to those in chapter 4) to keep in mind when designing open-ended critical thinking evaluation approaches. They will form the backdrop for the discussion of this chapter.   Keep in mind that we are offering

Table 5.1. General Guidelines for Designing
Open-ended Critical Thinking Evaluation Approaches

G1. Pilot your evaluation with a sample of students to make sure that it provides for them an interesting context as the basis of the reasoning task.

G2. In your pilot test, make explicit attempts to ensure that students understand the task or the questions in the way intended.

G3. As part of the task, seek justification from students for what they say and write.

G4. Be generous in interpreting students' responses, but not overly generous.

G5. Do not give credit merely because what students say is *true;* make sure that what they say is also *relevant* to the task as you described it.

G6. Look for patterns of strengths and weaknesses within individual student's responses and in responses from all students, and make note of these.

G7. Try to infer the presence and absence of critical thinking dispositions from what students say or write and from what they do *not* say or write, and make notes on your inferences and the evidence for them.

general guidelines, not strict rules. Therefore, they can be adjusted as the situation justifies.

With these guidelines provided, we now turn to a discussion of the first type of open-ended information-gathering techniques discussed in this chapter: short-answer critical thinking tests.

Short-answer Tests

These tests are suited to asking students to infer conclusions, to make credibility judgments, to identify assumptions, and to supply justifications for all three of these. In addition to the general guidelines in table 5.1, table 5.2 offers specific guides for the construction of short-answer tests.

We will illustrate the short-answer approach by examining a short-answer test designed to evaluate critical thinking in reading. Reading tasks provide ideal situations for gathering information

---

Table 5.2. Specific Guidelines for Designing
Short-Answer Tests

S1. Develop criteria for and an outline of a good response, based upon the aspects of critical thinking you wish to assess and suitable for the grade level being tested, but leave room for flexibility.

S2. When grading a student's response, first read the whole short answer without assigning a grade, in order to get an overview or sense of the student's response. Then reread it, applying the criteria you have developed.

S3. Do not allow such things as legibility, grammar, and spelling to influence unnecessarily your judgment of students' critical thinking; remember what you are testing.

S4. If students' responses differ from the ideal response, try to discern why. Do not mark responses merely right or wrong as in multiple-choice tests, and be open to legitimate alternative responses to the outline.

---

on students' critical thinking dispositions and abilities. To read well, a person must think well. In particular, a reader must be able to make inferences in order to interpret written text. In addition, several critical thinking dispositions are required to read well, including being open-minded, taking into account the total situation, trying to remain relevant to the main point, and looking for alternatives.

Consider the following examples from the Test of Inference Ability in Reading Comprehension devised by Linda M. Phillips for use in upper elementary school. Students are asked questions about three different stories which they read an episode at a time. They are told that to answer the questions they will have to use information given in the story and information they already know. They are warned that the story will not directly provide answers for the questions, so they will have to use both their common sense and the story. Here is the first episode from the story entitled "UFOs":

> Thousands of people around the world believe that they have seen unidentified flying objects. Anything in the sky that people do not understand may be called a UFO. People sometimes call UFOs "flying saucers," "spaceships from other planets," and "extraterrestrial spacecraft." Sometimes weather satellites, clouds, and bright stars are thought to be UFOs. Stories have been told that UFOs light up an area with many colored lights and that creatures of different sizes and colors have been seen in them. Another story was that UFOs drain power from any electrical sources in the immediate area. The weather, the time of day, and the number of people may make the UFO stories different.

This episode was designed in accord with the general guideline G1. The paragraph provides a context for the reasoning tasks which follow it, and in pilot studies the context was seen to be generally interesting to students at the upper elementary level.

The following short-answer questions provided the task for students and were designed to test their ability to make the sort of inferences required to comprehend the passage. They fall under topic 7b in the appendix, Explaining and Hypothesizing, and ask students to formulate hypotheses to account for things that are not explicitly accounted for in the text.

1. Why are UFOs sometimes called other names?

2. Why might anything in the sky which is not understood be called a UFO?

3. From where might UFOs come? Why do you say that?

4. Why may UFO stories be very different from each other?

Note that the questions are clear and direct, and through the word "why," they satisfy G3 by seeking justifications from students for what they write.

In accord with the specific guideline S1 for short-answer tests, we need a set of criteria for and an outline of good answers to the questions, taking into account the grade level of the students. Criteria for judging explanatory inferences can be found under topic 7b in the appendix. Here are four criteria based upon those in the appendix, modified slightly to suit the specific task at hand, reading a passage:

(1) the inference should explain what it is supposed to explain;

(2) inference should take account of all relevant textual information;

(3) the inference should be consistent with background knowledge the student can reasonably be expected to have;

(4) the inference should be better than the plausible alternatives.

Questions 1–4 are designed to test for students' ability to use these four criteria in making inferences from the information in the passage.

Here are good answers for the four questions, though not the only possible good answers:

1. UFOs are sometimes called other names because people name them according to their shape or probable origin.

2. Anything in the sky which is not understood might be called a UFO because people do not know what it is and the "U" stands for "unidentified."

3. UFOs might come from almost anywhere because things seen in the sky are often identified incorrectly.

4. UFO stories may differ from each other because people may see many kinds of objects in the sky and see them at various times and places.

These answers provide explanatory inferences that take account of all the relevant information contained in the paragraph, that are consistent with students' background knowledge, and that are better than alternatives. Besides testing for the ability to make explanatory inferences (topic 7b), this task can also serve to test for critical thinking dispositions. Dispositions listed in table 1.1 (page 12), which can be inferred from students' responses to these items, include taking into account the total situation and trying to remain relevant to the main point.

Let us now consider two other sets of answers to these four questions. The answers can be graded on a scale of 0 to 3. Student A's answers follow. Read the answers and assign what you think are fair grades. The student's actual words are printed in bold type.

Student A:

1. UFOs are sometimes called other names because **people know there are unidentified flying objects in the sky.**

2.   Anything in the sky which is not understood might
     be called a UFO because **that is the shape of
     whatever it is in the sky.**

3.   Although it is not known where UFOs come from,
     **they couldn't be from Earth because if they
     were people would know what they are.**

4.   UFO stories may be very different from each other
     because **people tend to exaggerate what they
     see and think of different names for UFOs.**

These answers reveal several problems in critical thinking. A general problem is that they fail to answer, or to answer fully, the questions asked. For example, the four questions ask for explanations of particular things, but the answers to the first three questions do not explain what was requested; they do not meet criterion 1. Answer 4 provides a possible explanation by suggesting that the different UFO stories came about because people thought of different names for UFOs. But this is not an adequate explanation because the student has not shown how the different names lead to different stories. People could tell the same stories even though they use different names for UFOs. Thus, the student's explanatory inferences fail to meet the first criterion of a purported explanation, namely, that it explain what it purports to explain. In what follows are our ratings for each item.

In item 1, the student failed to offer an explanation of why UFOs are sometimes called other names. It is not the case that the student offered an explanation that seems wrong or implausible, but that no explanation was offered at all. We would give the student 0 for this response.

In item 2, the student's answer lacks clarity because it is not clear to what shape the student is referring. Clarity, as discussed in chapter 1, must permeate decision making activities. In addition, the paragraph indicates that in calling something a UFO people take into account their beliefs about the origin of the object as well as the object's shape. Thus, applying criterion 2, the student's response has failed to take all the information into account. Again, we would assign a score of 0.

When you apply criterion 3 to item 3, the student's response seems to presuppose something which most elementary school children would know to be false: that anyone claiming to have seen a UFO would be able to recognize any earthly object which might be in the sky. We know, of course, that this is not true and most elementary school children could readily provide counterexamples to the claim. The student has failed to be sufficiently critical of the assumptions underlying the response. We would give a 0.

When you apply criteria 2 and 4, the answer to item 4 indicates that the student did not seem to consider alternatives nor take into account all of the information provided in the text. The possibility that UFO stories are different because people exaggerate what they see is, of course, real. However, the text provides clear suggestions of alternative explanations, and a student with a disposition to seek alternative explanations would likely recognize them. For instance, the text suggests that the explanation for the existence of different UFO stories may be related to the weather or to the time of day that a sighting was made. Our score is 0.

In discussing the student's response to each item, we also kept in mind guidelines S3 and S4. There were few, if any, problems with legibility, grammar, or spelling to distract our attention from the substance of the student's responses, but we remained alert to the possibility of this problem. We also made an effort to interpret the student's responses in terms of both critical thinking abilities and dispositions. In general, we feel that Student A's responses are poor and should be given zeros as we indicated. What do you feel? Why?

Student B's responses to the four questions follow. Using the guidelines, assign a grade to each response, based on a scale of 0 to 3.

Student B:

1. UFOs are sometimes called other names because **people don't know what to call them so they name them by shape.**

2. Anything in the sky which is not understood might be called a UFO because **that is what people call it when they jump to conclusions.**

3. Although it is not known where UFOs come from, **they could be from Earth because we have the materials and the people to build such craft.**

4. UFO stories may be very different from each other because **people may not be sure of what they see when they see different things in the sky.**

The student's answer to item 1 is fairly good. It satisfies criterion 1 at least partly by suggesting that UFOs come in different shapes and this fact accounts for the different names. When you apply criterion 2, however, this explanation can account for only part of the textual information. The answer is not able to explain the occurrence of such expressions as "from other planets" and "extraterrestrial" in the names people give. Such names do not connote the shape of UFOs but rather their possible origin. We would give the student credit for providing an explanation and for taking account of some of the textual information for a score of 2 out of the possible 3.

When you apply criterion 1 to item 2, the student's response may be a good one. People's tendency to jump to conclusions may account for why almost anything not understood is called a UFO. But the student has not remained sufficiently tentative. Applying criterion 4, an alternative response is that people call things UFOs for the very purpose of *not* jumping to conclusions. Calling an object a spaceship from another planet is jumping far quicker to a conclusion than is calling it an unidentified flying object. We would give the student 2 points for providing a plausible explanation, but withhold full credit because plausible alternatives are not mentioned.

The response to item 3 is partially acceptable because there certainly is the possibility that some or all UFOs could be made by human beings. The response satisfies criterion 1. However, the student appears to have failed to realize that since we do not know what UFOs are, we do not know whether we have the materials and the people to build them. The student has made an unwarranted claim that we have the materials and the skilled people. We would give 2 points.

The student's answer to item 4 is partially acceptable because, satisfying criterion 1, it presents one possible explanation of why UFO stories may be different from one another. The fact that people are uncertain of what they have seen can lead them to offer different stories. However, a possibility suggested in the text that the student seems to have failed to consider is that the observing conditions could also affect the stories people give. For example, seeing the same object in foggy compared to clear conditions, or in the daytime compared to the nighttime could lead to quite different accounts. So, the student's answer does not completely satisfy criterion 2 and does not satisfy criterion 4. We would give the student a score of 2.

In this section, we have shown how students' ability to make explanatory inferences can be tested in the context of reading a short passage about UFOs. Specifically, students can be tested on their ability to offer explanations that explain all they are supposed to explain, that are consistent with background knowledge the students can reasonably be expected to have, and that are better than plausible alternatives.

Using Argumentative Essays

An argumentative essay, as we shall use the term here, presents a thesis and uses reasons to defend it. That is, some statement is made about what to believe or do, and that statement is supported with reasons. The word "argumentative," like the word "critical," has negative and positive connotations in our language. To be argumentative can mean to be contentious, that is, to be likely to cause strife and conflict. To be argumentative can also mean to display a process of reasoning or to engage in reasoned discussion. It is in this *latter* sense that we shall use the term.

In general, an argumentative essay should make precisely clear the thesis that is to be defended. It should provide good reasons for assertions, credible sources of support where needed, and, when available, an explanation of how the reasons support the thesis being made (if this is not clear). When there are relevant alternative positions to the one being defended, there should be a fair presentation of these alternatives and an evaluation of their strengths and weaknesses compared to those of the thesis being defended. An argumentative essay should be presented in a clear and orderly manner.

Essays of this sort are particularly suitable for evaluating the coordination of a number of critical thinking abilities in working on a problem. To write a good argumentative essay, basic-support-related, inference-related, and clarity-related abilities must be used. In addition, the strategies and tactics involved in being orderly and in effectively communicating with an audience are needed.

Essays of this sort are also one of the best sources of evidence on students' critical thinking dispositions. It is possible to make inferences about students' critical thinking dispositions from the clarity of their thesis statements, the extent to which they defend them with good reasons, their use and mention of credible sources, and the orderliness of their essays.

Argumentative essays are less useful sources of detailed diagnostic information on specific areas of critical thinking. For example, in the Basic Support section of the appendix there are listed several criteria for judging the credibility of sources and observations. In most situations where such judgments are required, not all of the criteria are relevant. So, in order to acquire information on students' knowledge of all the criteria, several situations must be presented. Multiple-choice tests tend to be a better medium than essays for asking students to think about diverse situations in a reasonable amount of time.

When using argumentative essays to evaluate critical thinkng, most of the guidelines G1 to G7 and S1 to S4 are applicable, with appropriate adjustments for the type of task. In addition, we offer in table 5.3 broad guidelines for requesting and evaluating argumentative essays.

One of the most difficult problems in using argumentative essays is grading them. There is no way to specify precisely the

---

Table 5.3. Broad Guidelines for Requesting and Evaluating Argumentative Essays

E1. Pose a problem on which students can take and defend a position.

E2. Set the parameters of the essay: deadlines, length, and allowable consultation.

E3. Judge whether essays make clear statements of a thesis to be defended.

E4. Judge whether essays attend only to matters relevant to making and defending the thesis at issue.

E5. Judge the essays for proper use of evidence, sound inferences, and clear organization.

E6. Judge whether relevant alternative positions are fairly portrayed and evaluated.

E7. Judge whether due attention is given to such things as grammar, punctuation, and style.

ideal essay for making and defending a particular thesis. Usually, there is no one correct position to take or one proper way to defend it. So the grader must have general criteria for evaluating essays according to the *strength* of the reasoning they display rather than the particular conclusions that they reach. The seven guidelines, E1 to E7, provide no formula. The evaluator must exercise considerable judgment to follow them. This is why the use of argumentative essays requires an evaluator who is a critical thinker.

In the remainder of this section, we will describe a problem on which high school students might write an argumentative essay and suggest criteria for grading their essays. The particular problem was posed to high school students in the Second Annual University of Illinois College of Education Critical Thinking Essay Contest. High school students were asked to submit essays between 750 and 1200 words in length addressing the following problem:

> Several problems confronting teenagers have attracted public attention. Examples include alcohol abuse, other drug abuse, family relationships, sexuality and pregnancy, academic pressure, and gang membership. Other significant problems may also exist. What would you identify for concerned citizens as the most serious problem confronting teenagers in your community? Defend your position.

This task meets guidelines E1 and E2 and requires critical thinking. Students must consider a number of possible problems confronting teenagers in their communities and weigh and balance the seriousness of each. They must be able to explain why one problem is more serious than others, using and possibly developing criteria for making this judgment, and to identify this problem for some audience of "concerned citizens."

Table 5.4 is an adaptation of the scoring sheet used in grading the essays. It is a form for weighting and recording judgments made while following guidelines E3 to E7, so the numbers for these guidelines are contained in the table.

Table 5.4. Scoring Sheet for Argumentative Essays

For each judgment, assign scores from 0 to 3,
as follows:

0   =   very poor
1   =   poor
2   =   good
3   =   excellent

Judgment	Score
E3. *Judge whether the essay makes a clear state-* *ment of a thesis to be defended:*	_____

1. Is a conclusion clearly stated or implied?
   2. Are terms defined where necessary?
   3. Is equivocation and ambiguity avoided?	

E4. *Judge whether the essay attends only to* *matters relevant to making and defending* *the thesis at issue:*	_____

1. Does the essay discuss problems con-
      fronting teenagers?
   2. Is the problem one for the writer's
      community?
   3. Is it defended as the most serious problem?	

E5. *Judge the argument of the essay for proper* *use of evidence, sound inferences, and* *clear organization:*	_____
1. Sound inferences	

a.   Are the reasons sufficiently numerous
          and diverse?
      b.   Do conclusions follow from the reasons
          offered?	

Judgment	Score

   c. Are generalizations based on sufficient data?

   d. Do offered explanations account for the facts?

   e. Are value judgments based on acceptable principles?

  2. Proper use of evidence

   a. Are credible sources used?

   b. Is the offered evidence relevant?

  3. Clear organization

   a. Is it clear which conclusions reasons support?

   b. Are different issues kept separate?

   c. Are transitions between different points clear?

E6. *Judge whether relevant alternative positions are fairly portrayed and evaluated.*   _____

  1. Are alternative explanations recognized and evaluated

  2. Are apparent counterexamples evaluated?

E7. *Judge whether due attention is given in the essay to such things as grammar, punctuation, and style.*   _____

  1. Are grammatical principles followed?

  2. Is punctuation used properly?

  3. Are imagery and examples used effectively?

  4. Is the essay appropriate for the audience?

— — — — — — — — — — — — — — — —

  Total Score = The Sum of Scores for Each Judgment (Maximum = 15)   _____

The scoring guidelines presented in table 5.4 cannot be followed mechanically. An evaluator must understand critical thinking very well, no matter what the evaluation device being used, but this requirement is more obvious when judgments about complex matters must be made. For instance, before an essay can be rated on its use of credible sources, the evaluator must understand how the credibility of sources can be judged and how to make such judgments in context. We can provide no formulas or easy routes for making such judgments or for using argumentative essays for evaluating critical thinking. However, we suggest that a good way to improve your use of this type of critical thinking evaluation is to seek critical feedback from colleagues on evaluations you have made.

One suggestion is that you use the problem and the scoring sheet as practice. If possible, collaborate with some colleagues on grading some argumentative essays that students write about the problem. Try to resolve any differences in judgments that you reach, and then try the task with another group of essays to see whether you have reached better agreement. When you feel ready, pose another problem for students and adapt the scoring sheet as necessary.

Interviewing Individual Students

Interviewing a student individually is a way of acquiring very detailed information on the student's critical thinking. As with essay and short-answer tests, the general guidelines G1 to G7 should be followed. In addition, the advice contained in guidelines S1 to S4 for short-answer testing are also applicable, after making obvious alterations, since you will be dealing with oral rather than written discourse.

Interviewing students individually has certain advantages over other information-gathering techniques. First, many students can express their ideas far easier and more coherently in oral rather than in written form. While interviewing, the evaluator also has the option to ask students to clarify what they have said, to request further reasons for their conclusions, and to ask specific questions about what might have influenced their thinking. On the down side, some students do not like to be interviewed about their thinking, finding the situation threatening or embarrassing.

In addition to the guidelines already mentioned in previous sections, when interviewing students you should follow the guidelines in table 5.5.

We will illustrate interviewing using item 1 of the Test on Appraising Observations which was described in chapter 3. The item is set in the context of a traffic accident and describes what two witnesses to the accident say they saw. The task is to judge which of the witnesses is more credible.

> 1. A policeman is questioning Pierre and Martine. They were in their car at the intersection but were not in- volved in the accident. Martine is the driver and Pierre, who had been trying to figure out which way to go, is the map reader. The policeman asks Martine how many cars were at the intersection when the accident oc- curred. She answers, **"There were three cars."** Pierre says, "No, **there were five cars."**

The traffic accident context was found to be interesting to students in pilot studies of the test, satisfying guideline G1. Guideline S1 is satisfied by the following good response:

> Martine's statement is more credible because she was the driver and, therefore, would more likely be alert to the road and the traffic than Pierre, who was probably watching his map and the road signs. People who are more alert tend to be more credible.

There are three main elements of the ideal response: (1) the claim that Martine's statement is more credible; (2) the comparison of the perspectives of Martine and Pierre, which suggests she would be more alert to the road and the traffic; and (3) the state- ment of the general principle that people who are more alert to a situation tend to make more believable descriptions of it.

Table 5.5. Guidelines for Interviewing Students

I 1. Interview students one at a time. Try to set students at ease.

I 2. Tape record the interview session. Place the recorder and microphone in an unobtrusive place. To avoid distraction, allow the tape recorder to continue running while students are thinking but not speaking.

I 3. After the task is explained to the student, begin with an open-ended instruction such as: "I want you to tell me all that you are thinking as you work on the problem." If there are long periods of silence, probe open-endedly: "Can you tell me what you are thinking now?"

I 4. Only if the open-ended probe does not reveal the student's reasons, then ask: "Can you tell me why you chose the answer (or reached the conclusion) you did?"

I 5. Only if the direct question for reasons does not work, then ask a leading question, such as "Did such-and-such (referring to some factor in the problem situation) have anything to do with your thinking?"

I 6. Transcribe verbatim the taped interview onto paper.

Interviews were conducted in accord with the guidelines I1 to I6. The task was described to students, an example was provided, and students were asked whether they understood what to do. All this was done to meet guideline G2. Students were then directed to read the questions aloud and to say all that they were thinking while choosing their answers, in accord with I3. Here are verbatim transcriptions of two students working on item 1. Before reading beyond the transcriptions, decide what score you would give each student on a scale of 0 to 3.

> *Student 1*: (S = student; I = interviewer; . . . = pauses)
>
> S: Okay . . . I sort of go with . . . Well. um, I don't believe neither one because there was only one car, I guess. Despite, like, where it says, ah, they were in their car at the intersection but they were not involved in the accident. And Martine was driving and Pierre, I assume Pierre was with Martine, so there was only one car I'd say. But then there was, ah, the accident so probably there were three of them though . . . I got to go over this again . . .
>
> I: What sort of things are you thinking about? (Here, in response to the student's pause, the interviewer probed open-endedly in accord with guideline I3.)
>
> S: Well . . . they don't know which way to go and there were two stop signs. So there had to be a car this side and a car that side, right? So, and their car, that would make three cars, so I'd say it would be . . . the first one, I guess . . .
>
> I: Okay, go ahead.
>
> S: So, I pick the first one.
>
> I: Okay, go on to number 2.
>
> *Student 2:*
>
> S: Okay, well ah, I'd be more inclined to, ah . . . believe, ah, Martine because, ah, she's the driver. And Pierre, well, he's, he's trying to figure out which way to go by the maps. So he's not, that's trying to read a map and observe the place around him, right? He's not going to be able to compare to somebody who's paying attention to the road and . . . looking at where she's going.
>
> I: Okay, so go on to number 2.

In giving grades to the two students, we hope you tried to be guided by S2, S3, and S4, suitably modified for the interview context. You should have read each student's response completely before assigning a grade and tried to ignore such things as mode of expression and grammar when they did not interfere with understanding the students' thinking. Guideline S3 is especially important when grading interviews because transcriptions of oral communication often appear very disorganized. Finally, if you thought the students responded differently from the ideal response, you should have tried to discern why.

Both of these students were quite forthcoming in their responses. They said a lot and they provided a good indication of the basis of their reasoning. Had they not, the interviewer might have asked more leading questions in accord with I4 and I5, such as "Why do you think Martine's statement is more credible?" or "Did the fact that Pierre was reading the map make any difference to your thinking?"

Student 1 begins to answer by trying to support the claim that neither witness was credible. From the outset, the student considers a number of factors that might help to determine the number of cars that were at the intersection. Faltering, the student decides to go over the situation again.

In responding to the interviewer's probe, the student describes a line of reasoning leading to the conclusion that there were three cars at the intersection and that, therefore, Martine was more credible. In doing this, the student makes a number of unjustified assumptions: (1) "there were two stop signs," when the test says that there was an intersection with a stop sign in each direction; (2) "there had to be a car this side and a car that side," when there clearly did not have to be; and (3) "and their car, that would make three cars," when the situation allows that there might have been more than three. The student did not focus on the relevant difference between Martine's and Pierre's activities, nor infer that one would likely be more alert to the condition of the traffic while the other would be more alert to the map and direction signs. We would rate this student's thinking poor, possibly 0.

Student 2 makes a clear comparison between the roles of Martine and Pierre and how the roles interact with their observing. The third sentence is difficult to understand, but we would not take off points for this. Our interpretation is that Student 2 is saying that Pierre is reading the map and observing the place (not the road traffic) around him. The student's fourth sentence is stronger than is strictly justified; the student says that Pierre is not able to compare to Martine. The proper stance is that Pierre is *less likely* than Martine to observe the road conditions correctly. We can justifiably speak only of tendencies, not directly of Pierre and Martine, because we do not know enough about these people and the situation.

We would give the second student three points out of three. We would not deduct points for the unqualified comparison of Pierre and Martine, because the student has realized the essence of the difference in their observing positions. Also, we would not deduct points for the fact that the student did not abstract beyond the particular situation to the notion of alertness and its role in making observations more credible. It is rare and usually unnecessary that people give both the general principle and the particular facts of the situation in justifying their evaluations. The student has thought well and thus was given a good score. What do you think?

Monitoring Classroom Discussions

Teachers have considerable control over classroom discussions. Allowing students to engage in extended discussion about issues is a very effective means for developing the critical thinking dispositions and the critical thinking strategies and tactics as outlined in table 1.1 of chapter 1 and in the appendix. In this section we will concentrate on monitoring classroom discussions as a way to gather information on students' critical thinking abilities and dispositions.

Monitoring classroom discussions can be used to evaluate whether lessons specifically designed to encourage students' critical thinking abilities and dispositions are meeting their immediate goals. But this is not the only important use. The technique can be used longitudinally and regularly to compare students' progress over time. Thus, keeping a teacher journal as described in chapter 2 can be very useful in applying this technique. In addition, the technique can be used to examine lessons in which the teacher is not specifically prompting students to think critically, in order to see whether they apply the critical thinking which they learned in another context.

We will begin with a set of guidelines (table 5.6) for orchestrating and monitoring classroom discussions. The guidelines will be used to examine a lesson in American history to illustrate how a teacher might direct and monitor the classroom discussion during the lesson. The lesson is based on an American History course for senior high school written by Kevin O'Reilly. Students are presented a number of historical theories for the Great Depression. Here is one of them:

Historian A

When the stock crash took place in the last months of 1929, America plunged into its worst depression ever. The seeds for the depression lay in the seemingly prosperous American economy of the 1920's. For although the economy expanded in the '20's there were a number of weaknesses in it.

First, there were several weak industries in the 1920's, notably agriculture, textiles, and coal mining. Second, there was the phenomenon of technological unemployment. With more machines used to make goods, some workers were laid off. The result was that, although employment increased in the 1920's, it did not increase fast enough to keep up with the population growth. Even in the best years of the 1920's there were 1.5 million people unemployed. Third, the income of the country was concentrated more in the hands of the wealthy. The poor people did not share equally in the prosperity of the 1920's. Fourth, Americans experienced numerous foreign trade problems, especially with Europe, in the 1920's.

Table 5.6. Guidelines for Orchestrating and
Monitoring Classroom Discussions

D1. Ask questions whose answers require students to
     think critically. (See the appendix, topic 3.)

D2. Give students time to think before beginning their
     answers. (Giving students 10 seconds before
     answering provides considerable thinking time,
     but most teachers normally wait only about
     one second.)

D3. Do not dominate the discussion.

D4. Construct a checklist of questions to ask yourself
     about the students. (Are they being open-minded?
     Are they seeking reasons? Are they looking for
     alternatives? Are they taking into account the
     whole situation? Are their comments relevant to the
     main point? Are they taking and changing positions
     as the evidence warrants?)

D5. As soon as possible after the discussion, make
     journal notes on your answers to the questions
     in D4.

D6. Compare these notes to ones you made previously
     and make subsequently.

The teacher can use this historical explanation as the focus for a class or small group discussion. For instance, the merit of the explanation might be raised as the topic, and by monitoring what students say during the discussion, the teacher can gain information on students' critical thinking dispositions. If, for example, a student reminds the class that the discussion is getting off the topic of the explanation's merit, then this is evidence that the student is developing the disposition to remain relevant to the main point. In accord with guideline D5, this evidence can be recorded in a journal.

The discussion might be directed, in accord with guideline D1, by asking the following questions to test students' elementary clarification abilities listed in the appendix:

1. What is the main point of the passage?

2. What questions of clarification would you ask of Historian A?

3. What are some of the unstated reasons in Historian A's explanation?

In addition, students might be asked the following questions to gain information on their ability to judge inductions as set out in topic 7b of the appendix:

4. Does Historian A explain what he or she sets out to explain?

5. Are there other plausible explanations?

Consider, for example, question 1. Students tend to find it difficult to identify main points. Some of the difficulty seems to stem from their confusion of the main point of a passage with its topic. If in response to question 1, a student says, "The main point of the passage is the causes of the depression," then it seems the student is confusing the main point with the topic. In future classroom monitoring, note should be made of the prevalence of this confusion throughout the class.

Answers to question 4 must be interpreted carefully. Much depends upon the critical thinking sophistication and historical and economic knowledge of the students. For example, a student might affirm that Historian A has explained the depression because the historian provided four reasons why it occurred. If this student is not a sophisticated critical thinker, then such an answer might be judged adequate. For more sophisticated students, however, the answer might be taken to indicate poor critical thinking. A more sophisticated student might be expected to point out that the historian has not really stated the links between the factors mentioned and the occurrence of the depression. What is the link, for instance, between the trade problems with Europe and the onset of the depression? Given that such links are not stated, the sophisticated critical thinker could be given credit for saying that Historian A has not explained the Great Depression and for defending that judgment on the grounds of the historian's failure to make explicit links in the argument. A journal should contain records of the degree of sophistication displayed by students in their judgments of explanations.

Monitoring a classroom discussion thus allows the teacher to reach conclusions about students' critical thinking which multiple-choice testing does not reveal. In particular, the teacher can discover whether students are interpreting the task as intended and whether differences in critical thinking sophistication help account for differences in students' answers.

The model for collecting information on students' critical thinking in history, which we see in the approach based upon O'Reilly's historical explanations, is very valuable. The value lies in the flexibility of the approach and the breadth of information provided on students' critical thinking abilities and dispositions. In addition, the approach allows information on critical thinking to be gathered when students are working on a more complex problem than is found in most commercially available tests.

Also, since the issue is one for which there is not likely to be one answer upon which everyone can settle, students should display the critical thinking dispositions to be open-minded, to seek alternatives, and so on, which the mentally prepared teacher can recognize. The teacher can also note whether students use good judgment in making decisions in the face of incomplete information, and use their critical thinking in working with other people. These aspects of critical thinking cannot be tested at all in multiple-choice approaches and probably not easily in essay and short-answer testing.

The approach can be expanded to examine students' critical thinking in lessons which do not explicitly encourage their critical thinking. For instance, without asking whether a historical passage explains what it purports to explain, the teacher may monitor a classroom discussion about the passage to see whether students think to raise this issue themselves. In this way, the teacher can acquire some idea of how much effect the critical thinking instruction is having.

Chapter Summary

In this chapter we have provided some guidelines and examples for designing four open-ended approaches for gathering information on students' critical thinking: using short-answer critical thinking tests, using argumentative essays, interviewing individual students as they work on problems, and carefully monitoring classroom discussions. We began with seven general guidelines which apply to each of the open-ended approaches. In abbreviated form they are as follows:

G1. Provide an interesting context.

G2. Ensure that students understand the task.

G3. Seek justification for what students say and write.

G4. Be generous in interpreting students' responses.

G5. Distinguish truth from relevance in students' responses.

G6. Look for patterns of strengths and weaknesses.

G7. Look for evidence of critical thinking dispositions.

We provided four guidelines specific to the short-answer approach and illustrated their application in a short-answer test of reading for the middle school grades. The guidelines are:

S1. Develop criteria and outlines of ideal
responses.

S2. Read the whole short answer before grading.

S3. Remember what you are testing.

S4. Try to discern why students answer as
they do.

We illustrated how to request an argumentative essay using as topic "The most serious problem confronting teenagers in the writer's community." We provided a scoring guide for grading the essays and the following guidelines for using argumentative essays:

E1. Pose a problem on which students can take
and defend a position.

E2. Set clear parameters for the essay.

E3. Judge whether there is a clear statement of a
thesis to be defended.

E4. Judge whether attention is devoted only to
relevant issues.

E5. Judge the use of evidence, inferences, and
organization.

E6. Judge whether alternatives are fairly
portrayed and evaluated.

E7. Judge such things as grammar, punctuation,
and style.

The guidelines for essay and short-answer testing are also applicable to interviewing individual students, when allowance has been made for the oral rather than written context. We illustrated the use of interviewing in the context of appraising eyewitness testimony and suggested the following additional five guidelines specific to this approach:

I1. Try to set students at ease.

I2. Tape record the interview session.

I3. Begin with a nonleading instruction.

I4. Only then, seek justification explicitly.

I5. Only then, ask leading questions.

I6. Transcribe verbatim the taped interview.

Finally, we provided guidance and examples of monitoring classroom discussions as a means of gathering information on students' critical thinking abilities and dispositions. We chose a lesson in American history at the high school level for illustration. We recommended six guidelines for this approach:

D1. Ask questions which require students to think critically.

D2. Give students time to think.

D3. Do not dominate the discussion.

D4. Construct a checklist of questions about the class.

D5. Make journal notes soon after class.

D6. Compare these notes to ones made previously and subsequently.

The approaches described in this chapter complement the multiple-choice testing described in chapter 4. Multiple-choice testing cannot provide information on dispositions, but essays, interviewing, and classroom monitoring can. Multiple-choice tests can provide detailed information on specific aspects of critical thinking ability, but the open-ended approaches cannot easily provide such detail.

We have necessarily focused on only a narrow range of examples. We encourage you to look for the general lessons among the particulars and to use these lessons in application to your own needs.

Suggested Readings

Costa, A., Ed. (1985). *Developing Minds: A Resource Book for Teaching Thinking, Part X.* Association for Supervision and Curriculum Development, 225 N. Washington Street, Alexandria, VA 22314.

O'Reilly, K. (1985). *Critical Thinking in American History: Book 4, Spanish-American War to Vietnam.* Critical Thinking Press, 775 Bay Road, South Hamilton, MA 01982.

Phillips, L. (1987). *The Design and Development of the Phillips-Patterson Test of Inference Ability in Reading Comprehension.* Institute for Educational Research and Development, Memorial University of Newfoundland, St. John's, Newfoundland, Canada, A1B 3X8.

——— and Norris, S. (1987). Reading well is thinking well. In Burbules (Ed.), *Philosophy of Education, 1986.* Normal, IL: The Philosophy of Education Society, 187-197.

CHAPTER SIX

MAKING DECISIONS FROM INFORMATION GATHERED ON STUDENTS' CRITICAL THINKING

In chapter 4 we briefly discussed several purposes which you might have in evaluating students' critical thinking. Usually, the purpose of evaluation is to make one of three types of decisions: (1) about placement, grading, diagnosis, and remediation of students; (2) about the effectiveness of teachers, programs, and methods; and (3) about the development of programs and methods.

As you might infer from the second and third purposes, the information gathered on students' critical thinking is not always used to make decisions about them. Sometimes, information on students' critical thinking is a major factor in the evaluation of something else—a program, a teacher, a school, etc.

However, whatever the decision being made, the information on students' critical thinking must meet at least two conditions:

Condition 1—the information gathered on students' critical thinking must be high quality, that is, it must accurately reflect their critical thinking; and

Condition 2—the information must be sufficient for ruling out plausible, competing decisions that might be made.

Chapters 2 to 5 dealt with various issues related to gathering quality information on students' critical thinking, such as general indicators of quality, choosing a commercial critical thinking test, and making your own multiple-choice or open-ended information-gathering techniques. These latter four chapters have thus, directly or indirectly, dealt with condition 1.

The purpose of this chapter is to discuss condition 2. Specifically, in order for the information you gather to rule out competing decisions to the decision you wish to make, particular attention must be paid to the sort of information to gather on students' critical thinking and to how to gather it.

We will discuss separately the three types of decisions mentioned above, even though they are not mutually exclusive. It is possible that, for example, information on students' critical thinking could be used both to guide the development of curriculum materials and to judge the effectiveness of those materials in critical thinking instruction. The three types of decisions do not include all the possible ones that might rely on information about students' critical thinking. For example, the information might be used for testing theories of human reasoning and for setting policy regarding the goals of education.

Section One: Placement, Grading, Diagnosis, and Remediation

There is a widespread view that we should regard highly all student attempts at reasoning. We can agree with the sentiment expressed in this view, if the aim is to avoid bringing students immediately to task for every mistake they make. There is certainly a sense in which people learn by themselves from their own mistakes. So students should be encouraged to think about situations, be allowed to make mistakes, and be given the time to see for themselves the inadequacy of their thinking.

However, people also learn from others, and we believe that teachers would be remiss in their duties if they did not help students see errors or inadequacies in their thinking and ways of doing better. The concept of critical thinking presented in chapter 1 is based on the idea that not all thinking is equally good. Human experience has shown that some thinking is better than others, and students should be able to profit in a direct and efficient manner from this experience. Therefore, students should be given direct instruction in critical thinking and their mistakes in thinking pointed out to them. However, once evaluation focuses on particular individuals, any information collected must be of especially high quality and used extremely judiciously. We offer the following suggestions.

1. We recommend for placing, grading, and diagnosing individual students that at least some of the information on their critical thinking be collected one-on-one, student and evaluator.

One reason for recommending this approach is to help ensure that condition 1 is met, that is, that the information gathered accurately reflect students' critical thinking. Another reason is to help pinpoint the best instructional decisions. For example, suppose a multiple-choice critical thinking test is administered to students in a group testing format. On the basis of scores on the test, conclusions about the remediation needed by individual students will be made. Suppose James answered incorrectly most of the questions on judging the credibility of sources. Based upon this fact, one might conclude that James needs extra instruction in the criteria for judging credibility and in their application. Two questions can now be asked related to the two conditions above: (1) does the information gathered give an accurate indication of James's ability to judge the credibility of sources; and (2) given that the information is accurate, does it rule out competing conclusions to the one that James needs remediation?

Assume that, after consideration, it is concluded that the information gathered is indeed an accurate indication of James's ability. That is, let us assume that condition 1 is satisfied. We can now go on to consider condition 2. Satisfying this condition requires that we rule out competing interpretations of James's performance. The proposed conclusion is that James needs help with criteria for judging credibility. However, perhaps this is not the case at all. Suppose James's teacher has consistently equated the truth of people's statements with the credibility of those state-

162 EVALUATING CRITICAL THINKING

ments. If this is the case, a plausible alternative interpretation of James's poor performance is that he makes credibility judgments solely on the basis of his prior beliefs about the truth of the statements judged. As long as this interpretation is plausible, then it is not justified to conclude without qualification that James' poor performance was due solely to his not knowing criteria for credibility judgment. Another plausible conclusion exists, namely, that James does not really understand the task. If James had met one-on-one with the evaluator and been asked to explain his choice of answers, his confusion and its source might have been revealed.

2. We recommend that information be gathered on the extent of students' critical thinking dispositions as well as their critical thinking abilities.

To do this, more substantial tasks than those found on multiple-choice tests should be used. For example, essay tests can provide information on whether students are disposed to seek reasons, try to remain relevant to the main point, look for alternatives, and so on. Sometimes the problem with students' thinking is that they just do not try to think critically, not that they are unable to do so; therefore, dispositions are important to evaluate.

3. We recommend collecting information in a number of modes: oral, written, and discussion.

In addition to the standard way of administering commercial multiple-choice tests, these instruments can often be adapted for oral administration. Students should also be given a chance to write, because abilities to think critically in oral and written expression are both important, but not necessarily equal to nor indicative of one another. So constructed-response testing should also be used. Also, starting a discussion for the purpose of gathering information is useful. Some individuals are able to think well in an interactive discussion situation, but do not do well when they are writing or speaking alone, and ability to think critically while interacting with other people is an important aspect of critical thinking.

Section Two: Decisions about Effectiveness

Decisions about effectiveness are the concern of many evaluations of critical thinking. Consider the following questions:

1. Are my students learning enough about how to think critically?

2. Should I provide more examples during my critical thinking instruction?

3. Is the XYZ critical thinking program better than the ABC program?

4. Which students would benefit most from taking the critical thinking course?

5. Is our school meeting the guidelines of the school system in providing critical thinking instruction?

6. Are the schools in our system adequately preparing students with the critical thinking skills they will need to work in a complex society?

7. Would instruction in critical thinking in each school subject be more effective than a specialized course in critical thinking?

8. Should schools in our nation place more emphasis on critical thinking instruction than they have in the past?

All of these questions are about effectiveness: of critical thinking instruction in general, of providing more examples in critical thinking instruction, of two critical thinking programs, and of giving critical thinking instruction in each school subject compared to a specialized course in critical thinking.

An interesting and important fact is that gathering information on students' critical thinking is necessary to answering completely each question. Even when the students themselves are not the focus of the evaluation, they are still the ones directly tested. Question 1 queries how much students are learning to think critically. Therefore, in order to answer the question, information on students' critical thinking is needed. Question 2 contains an implicit reference to the efficacy of providing examples in teaching critical thinking. Information on students' critical thinking is also necessary to answering fully this question. Question 6 refers to the effect of certain schools in preparing students with the critical thinking skills needed to live in a complex society, and question 4 refers to the effect of a particular critical thinking program on the critical thinking of different types of students. Answering completely both questions 6 and 4 requires information on students' critical thinking.

For illustration of how a decision about effectiveness might be made, let us focus upon question 3 and see how answers to the question might be sought. The question focuses on the relative effectiveness of two critical thinking programs: Is the XYZ critical thinking program better than the ABC program?

Let us suppose that the XYZ program is one that purports to teach generalizable critical thinking skills, that is, those which are supposed to apply across all school subjects as well as out of school contexts. The ABC program, however, is based on the belief that thinking critically is different for each subject area and that, therefore, critical thinking must be taught differently in each school subject.

(There currently is considerable debate about this issue. There are those who argue that to separate critical thinking instruction from subject matter as is done by the XYZ program is to falsely assume that critical thinking can make sense outside of particular subjects. Critical thinking, these people maintain, is nothing other than good thinking in the subject in question, meaning that good thinking in science is different from good thinking in literature, is different from good thinking in history, and so on. Others argue that a generalized course would be more effective because there are general critical thinking abilities and dispositions which can be taught outside of as well within the context of any subject, but which are applicable to each subject and to contexts outside the domain of school subjects. The XYZ program attempts to teach such generalizable abilities and dispositions. We stated in chapter 1 that this second position is the one we hold.)

In this section, we wish to examine the design of an *evaluation experiment* that would provide some evidence on which of the two programs is more effective. We stated at the beginning of this chapter that the information on students' critical thinking used in an evaluation must be sufficient for ruling out plausible, competing decisions. Therefore, the aim in designing the evaluation experiment is to rule out plausible, competing conclusions that something other than the differences in XYZ and ABC is the reason for any differences found in the students' critical thinking.

We cannot in this book provide very much or very sophisticated information on experimental design. Our purpose is, rather, to sensitize those who have not encountered these issues to the fact that making decisions about effectiveness is quite a complex task. We will highlight some considerations which must be made and the rationale for them. However, in actual practice you should seek expert advice.

>> *Implementing the treatment*

"Treatment" is a term used in educational experiments to refer to the program or procedure that is being studied. The treatment in an experiment might be a course, whose effect on student achievement is under scrutiny. It might be a teaching methodology, whose effectiveness in increasing student participation in classroom discussion is being studied. Making sure that the treatment is actually implemented correctly is an important step in a successful experiment.

Suppose that the XYZ program is tried in some classrooms, but the students showed no improvement in their scores on the test that was used to study the program's effectiveness. The conclusion might be suggested that the program is ineffective. However, before this conclusion can be accepted without qualification, competing conclusions must be eliminated. One possible reason for the lack of increase in scores is that the program was not implemented correctly by the teachers. This might be due to their being provided too little inservice instruction in the philosophy and objectives of the program and in the actual content to be taught. Until this conclusion can be ruled out, we cannot assume that there is a link between the lack of improvement in students' critical thinking and the effectiveness or ineffectiveness of the XYZ program.

>> *The need for comparative information*

If question 3 is to be answered, some comparative information needs to be gathered in order to determine the relative effectiveness of the critical thinking programs. Several sorts of comparisons are possible: among the perceptions of teachers, students, and parents of the effectiveness of the program they experienced; between the observations of the atmosphere of classes using both programs; of the degree of student involvement in questioning and discussion; of the degree of interest and motivation displayed by both teachers and students; or between the scores of students in the different programs on some test of critical thinking. Alternatively, information of each of the above sorts might be collected and question 3 answered on the basis of all the comparisons. The point, however, is that some sort of comparative information must be collected.

>> *Controlling an experiment*

Suppose the information collected to help answer question 3 is students' performances on The Ennis-Weir Critical Thinking Essay Test. Suppose, in addition, that the information meets the standards of quality discussed in previous chapters, that is, that condition 1 is satisfied. We want to know whether the information can provide the sort of comparison needed to answer question 3. Suppose that the students who took the XYZ course had been specially selected for the course on the basis of their high grade point averages, and that the students who took the ABC course received no special screening. If this were the case, we would all agree that the comparison between the scores of the two groups does not provide legitimate information for answering question 3. The evaluation experiment does not provide information that satisfies condition 2 because it fails to rule out the plausible, competing explanation that any differences in scores are due to the differences in students and not to differences in effectiveness of the programs. We would say that the experiment *needs to be controlled* for prior differences in students' grade point averages.

Consider an evaluation with the purpose of judging the effectiveness of a science teacher's instruction in critical thinking. The students in the teacher's science class are given a test of critical thinking at the beginning of the semester and another one at the end. Scores are compared and it is found that the students score 20% higher at the end of the semester. The conclusion is reached that the teacher is effective in teaching critical thinking.

Is this conclusion legitimate? An alternative conclusion is that the 20% increase in students' scores would have occurred even if the teacher had not been making a special effort to teach critical thinking. Perhaps this size of increase can be expected just from the students' being several months older, or from some other educational experience the students have had. Unless these competing conclusions can be shown to be wrong, then it is not correct to conclude that the increase in students' scores is a result of the teacher's instruction, because we cannot be sure that there is a link between the teacher's instruction and the students' critical thinking. The trial has not been controlled for student maturation and experiences other than the teacher's instruction.

Control is exercised in an experiment when, through the design used, certain factors are ruled out as plausible, competing explanations of the experimental results. Suppose that one grade ten class of students studied critical thinking using the XYZ program and that another studied the ABC program. At the end of each, students were given the Ennis-Weir test and the result was that the average score for the students in the ABC program was 21 and the average score for those in the XYZ was 6. One explanation of this result is that the ABC program is more effective than the XYZ program. However, suppose that the students who took the ABC program were better critical thinkers from the outset. Then this experiment does not control for the critical thinking ability of the students. Therefore, a plausible, competing explanation of the experimental result is that there was no difference in the effectiveness of the programs, but that the result was caused by the difference in student critical thinking ability that was there from the outset.

Controlling Student Factors. In order to rule out the competing explanation that the result was caused by differences in students' critical thinking that were present from the outset, the experiment should control for students' initial ability in critical thinking. To do this, the evaluator should make sure that students in each group have at the outset equivalent, or nearly equivalent, critical thinking abilities. Equality can be sought in a number of ways. One way is to select or make groups whose average abilities on many school subjects are equivalent. One might assume that if the groups are equal in everything else, then they should also be equal in critical thinking. If one is hesitant to make this assumption, then students' scores on some critical thinking test might be used to assign students to groups such that the average critical thinking score of each group is the same. Alternatively, students can be assigned randomly to each group. Using an alphabetical list of all the students' names, for instance, the odd-numbered students could be put into one group and even-numbered into the other.

If there is no freedom to assign students randomly to groups because they must remain in their normal classes, then a decent experiment cannot be conducted using two classes of students, unless the classes happen to be equivalent in critical thinking. If intact classes must be used, it usually is better to use several classes. If five or six classes can be taught each critical thinking program, then classes can be assigned to use one program or another in such a way that the average critical thinking ability of the classes in one group is about the same as the average for classes in the other. If this is so, the experiment is fairly well controlled.

Overall, the most effective approach to controlling student factors is random assignment of individual students to groups. Any other approach leaves many possibilities for competing explanations to arise. For example, even if the groups in an experiment are controlled for their critical thinking ability by using scores on a test, there might be differences in the motivation of students in each group. If this is so, then these differences in motivation might plausibly be the cause of any differences in the final experimental results. This problem would be avoided by random assignment. However, when random assignment to groups is not possible, alternate approaches as mentioned above are available.

Controlling Classroom Factors. Suppose an experiment comparing the effectiveness of the XYZ and the ABC programs is controlled for student factors. The Ennis-Weir test is administered at the end of each program and the results are those given above: the average score for students in the ABC program is 21 and, for the XYZ program, 6. Could we say now that the ABC program is better than the XYZ program without finding plausible, competing explanations of the results? The answer is probably not, if classroom factors have not been controlled.

Classroom factors are numerous and include number of students, available time for instruction, and physical resources. Suppose that the class which used the ABC program had far fewer students in it; had considerably more time available for instruction; or had greater access to resources such as books, magazines, and computers. Then it is plausible that it was not the different program but the difference in one or several of these classroom factors that caused the difference in the experimental results. It is plausible, for instance, that critical thinking instruction would be facilitated in classes with fewer students. Therefore, if there were fewer students in the class taking the ABC program, then this fact might account for the difference in the results.

Classroom factors that might affect the results of the experiment should be identified and controlled. Sometimes, however, this may be difficult in a school context. The number of students in a class may not be easy to adjust, for example. This fact may preclude doing the experiment at all, or it may simply mean that the results of the experiment will need to be taken more tentatively.

Controlling Teacher Factors. Suppose that all relevant student and classroom factors in an experiment are controlled. If the same differences reported above were still observed (ABC average 21, XYZ average 6), would any other plausible, competing explanations of the test results exist (besides the explanation that the difference in program caused them)? Well, suppose that the teacher using the ABC program was much more experienced than the one using the XYZ program and had taught critical thinking before. Then, the cause of the differences found in the experiment might be the difference in the teachers' experience. Evaluation experiments must therefore control for teacher factors. The teachers involved with each of the programs should be relatively equal in relevant characteristics, such as their training, experience, and rapport with students.

It is often difficult to find two teachers with similar enough characteristics to gain the required sort of experimental control. When this is the case, the evaluation cannot rely on only two classes for information. Several classes would need to try each program, and an attempt should be made to equalize the average characteristics of teachers assigned to teach each program.

>> *Section summary*

It should be clear from the previous discussion that if questions of effectiveness such as question 3 are asked, then the experiment designed to answer the questions must take several complex issues into account. First, the experiment should be designed to ensure that the treatment being studied is implemented as desired. For example, if the treatment is a new course, then that course should be taught the way the developers intended. Second, the experiment should collect comparative information because evaluations of effectiveness attempt to judge the effectiveness of one thing compared to another. Third, one of the most important concerns is that the experiment be controlled. In general, in an experiment whose results can be affected by student-related, classroom-related, and teacher-related factors, a simple design involving a few classrooms of students will not give good results. Serious evaluation of critical thinking effectiveness is difficult to do, requires the cooperation of many people, and requires expert evaluators. There is no way around these facts.

Section Three: Developmental Uses

Evaluation of students' critical thinking can play an important role in the development of programs for teaching critical thinking, in the development of methods for teaching critical thinking, and in the professional development of teachers.

>> *Program and methods development*

In the development of new programs and teaching techniques, information gathered on students' critical thinking can be used as feedback. Suppose students complete a pilot-phase history unit on assessing the credibility of sources and are tested on their ability to judge the credibility of some historical sources. If the information was detailed in that it examined separately many of the principles of critical thinking which play a role in judging credibility, then needed changes in the unit could possibly be pinpointed. Similarly, information on students' performance in analyzing arguments could be used to judge the usefulness of instruction in deduction, let us say, in teaching students how to analyze lines of reasoning.

The points about experimental design covered in the previous section should not be forgotten when information on students' critical thinking is used for developmental purposes. Many developmental questions rely on knowledge of the effectiveness of what is being developed because one criterion for judging whether to keep, modify, or discard the unit on the credibility of historical sources would be the effectiveness of the unit in teaching this aspect of critical thinking. One must be alert to the presence of plausible, competing explanations of the information other than the quality of the unit itself. Maybe the unit is good, but has been given a poor trial by an incompetent teacher. Maybe the unit is poor, but has been supplemented by a highly skilled teacher of critical thinking. Maybe the unit is poor, but the students who tried it were exceptionally smart and performed well despite the poor quality unit.

>> *Professional development*

Information on students' critical thinking is used for professional development when a teacher or a group of cooperating teachers collects the information for use in self-improvement. A teacher's students are not faring as well as desired in critical thinking. The teacher examines his or her approach, makes some changes, and collects further information. If there is improvement, the teacher might incorporate the changes into his or her repertoire. If there is no improvement, other changes might be tried.

In using information for this purpose, the teacher cannot depend on experimental control. For example, the teacher cannot afford to say that since this year's group of students is different from last year's group, I cannot make any sound decisions about the effectiveness of the approach I used last year compared to the approach I used this year. The teacher cannot afford to demand experimental control because he or she *must* act now, that is, must teach in some way now, and must try to improve continuously.

Instead of experimental control the teacher has another tool: *multiple observations using a variety of information-gathering techniques over an extended period*. Observations can be made using such techniques as formal tests, monitoring classroom discussions, and seeking verbal feedback from students on what they find effective. If observations made using a variety of techniques lead to similar results, then they can generally be trusted more than observations made using only one technique. In addition, if observations concur over a period of time, then greater trust can be placed in them. Thus, a teacher can compensate for not being able to effect true experimental control over the factors that might influence students' performance.

Chapter Summary

An evaluation dealing with some aspect of critical thinking not only must be concerned with the collection of quality information, but also with how that information is used. When information is to be used for the diagnosis and remediation of particular individuals, then we suggest that a variety of detailed information on both abilities and dispositions be collected on the individuals and that at least some of this information be collected in one-on-one situations.

When the concern is with making decisions about effectiveness of teachers, programs, schools, or whatever, then the evaluator must meet the standards of experimental design. In short, these standards involve making sure the treatment is implemented as intended, setting up the proper sort of comparison, and controlling the experiment for extraneous student-related, classroom-related, and teacher-related factors.

Developmental uses often do not warrant meeting the standards of experimental design. Sometimes, there is not more than one plausible explanation of the results of the treatment, as in the trial of a very short unit of work. At other times, control is impossible or practically impossible, as when a teacher is seeking feedback on his or her teaching techniques. In such situations we suggest looking for concurrence among observations using a variety of information-gathering techniques over an extended time period.

Suggested Readings

Cronbach, L. (1982). *Designing Evaluations of Educational and Social Programs.* San Francisco: Jossey-Bass.

Tomko, T. and Ennis, R. (1980). Evaluation of informal logic competence. In Blair and Johnson (Eds.), *Informal Logic: The First International Symposium.* Inverness, CA: Edgepress, 113-144.

CHAPTER SEVEN

SUMMARY AND CONCLUDING REMARKS

The main point of this book can be summarized concisely: evaluating critical thinking is an activity that itself requires thinking critically. In practice, this means that when evaluating critical thinking you should

1. have in mind a clearly specified and well justified notion of critical thinking;

2. understand what contributes to quality information on students' critical thinking;

3. be careful not to accept automatically the technical notions of reliability and validity as indicators of quality;

4. know how to choose from among commercial critical thinking tests those that most suit your purpose;

5. know how to devise tests and other indicators of critical thinking that avoid serious and common pitfalls;

6. use quality information on students' critical thinking that suits the purpose and is in accord with the standards either of experimental research, in particular, or critical thought, in general.

What is Critical Thinking?

Critical thinking is a complex organization of many things: clarity-related abilities, inference-related abilities, basic support-related abilities, abilities to use strategies and tactics, and a set of dispositions which comprise a critical spirit. In chapter 1 we identified the central core of critical thinking as reasonable and reflective thinking that is focused upon deciding what to believe or do. From this core we described a detailed specification of the abilities and dispositions which are required in order to engage in such reasonable and reflective thought.

The definition meets a number of general requirements that any suggested definition of critical thinking ought to satisfy. First, the definition finds a fair degree of agreement among educators. The definition maintains that critical thinking is comprised of both abilities and dispositions and the definition is useful for both basic research and practical educational needs. Our belief is that critical thinking abilities and dispositions as we have defined them are applicable to all school subjects and to a wide variety of activities outside school that require good thinking. In order to become a good critical thinker, we believe that the abilities and dispositions must be displayed by teachers and practiced by students in a large number and variety of contexts.

Second, our notion of critical thinking provides a defensible educational ideal. To become a critical thinker in the sense we have portrayed implies a transformation of character that falls clearly within the ideals of Western education: critical thinkers are autonomous decision-makers, open-minded to the fallibility of their own views and to the value of other's views, and creative in the formulation of ideas. These characteristics are not all we associate with being educated, but they are important features.

Third, because of the detailed list of topics which we have provided in the appendix, the definition is useful for guiding instruction, curriculum development, and evaluation. The usefulness of the definition for evaluation lies in part in its provision of content specifications for critical thinking tests or other techniques for gathering information on critical thinking.

Fourth, while the definition includes principles for guiding decisions of what to believe or do, it also provides room for, and even demands, the application of good judgment. Thus, there is no intimation that thinking that leads to decisions about belief and action can be automatized. This, we believe, is in accord with the intuitions of most educators. Many important decisions are just too complex to specify completely how they should be made.

Quality Information on Students' Critical Thinking

An evaluation of students' critical thinking relies fundamentally on the quality of the information which is gathered on their thinking. In the evaluation field there are two indicators of quality—reliability and validity. Technically, reliability is the consistency of the information that a technique provides. Validity is the extent to which a test measures what it is supposed to measure in a specified situation.

The technical notion of reliability is not the same as the everyday notions associated with this word. Reliability in its technical sense is the consistency of the information gathered, whereas in its everyday sense it is trustworthiness. There is overlap between the notions, but they do not mean the same thing. Information that is reliable in the technical sense cannot necessarily be trusted to mean what it seems to mean. In addition, some estimates of reliability employed in the field of evaluation are really measures of how well pieces of information correlate with one another; for example, how well the items on a test correlate with each other. A low reliability computed using this technique may actually be good in critical thinking evaluation, because there may be very good reasons for expecting some items on a critical thinking test not to correlate with one another.

Validity means roughly the same as the everyday sense of reliability—trustworthiness. More precisely, a test is valid in a situation to the extent that it measures what it is supposed to measure in that situation. Important features of the situation include the background knowledge and abilities of the students.

Choosing a Commercial Test

There is not a lot of choice in commercially available critical thinking tests. Most of them are in multiple-choice format and test for critical thinking in the context of general knowledge. No test examines all aspects of critical thinking and no test examines all that is possible within any given aspect of critical thinking. This is not a criticism, but reflects the tremendous breadth of critical thinking. There is also a wide spread in the quality of available tests, so the consumer should be aware of how quality should be judged.

Because of the narrow range of choice, the evaluator of critical thinking in the context of general knowledge may have to resort to devising his or her own information-gathering devices. The evaluator of critical thinking in specific subjects will have to be careful in selecting from what is available. We have not analyzed the availability of such tests in this book, but suggest making judgments using the same sort of guidelines outlined in chapter 3 and listed again below. In any case, if critical thinking *dispositions* are the focus of concern, then the available multiple-choice tests will probably be of no help.

To guide the evaluator in choosing from among available critical thinking tests, we offer the following general guidelines:

1. Pay close attention to the directions, the items, and the scoring guide.

2. Take the test yourself, and compare your answers with those of the guide.

3. Satisfy yourself that the scoring guide is reasonable, but do not expect to agree with it completely for any but deduction items.

4. Ask yourself often, "Does this really test for some aspect of critical thinking?"

5. For purported comprehensive critical thinking tests, ask yourself, "Does this cover enough of critical thinking in a balanced manner to be called a comprehensive critical thinking test?"

6. For purported aspect-specific critical thinking tests ask yourself, "Does this cover enough of the aspect?"

7. Read the test manual and note the statistical information, but remember that test publishers have a conflict of interest in deciding what information to include and exclude.

These guides are general, as we said. They provide no formula for choosing among tests. In particular, they are no replacement for the careful judgment of a person knowledgeable of critical thinking and educational evaluation.

Making Your Own Multiple-choice Tests

When there is no commercially available test suitable to your purpose, you may wish to construct your own. In chapter 4 we offered some advice on constructing multiple-choice tests for four aspects of critical thinking: deduction, credibility, induction, and assumption identification. Our primary rule in test construction is that you pay close attention to the meaning of the questions you devise and of the interpretations you place on students' responses to them. A major problem to keep in mind is that differences in students' background beliefs and their levels of critical thinking sophistication can result in their thinking well but choosing answers other than those keyed correct.

In order to minimize problems with multiple-choice items, we make the following suggestions:

1. Use the comparative-judgment approach for credibility, induction, and assumption-identification items.

2. Use the noncomparative-judgment approach for deduction items.

3. Provide as much context as is permitted by the reading load.

4. Interview examinees who are like the target examinees in order to see what sorts of background beliefs and levels of sophistication they bring to the items.

5. Add an item that offers possible justifications for the options in the original item, but be aware that you might be giving examinees ideas they would not otherwise have.

6. Add an open-ended request to examinees to explain why they answered as they did.

7. Be well informed about critical thinking and the topic of the item, whether it be general knowledge or some specific school subject.

8. Beware of the different threads of meaning associated with the term, "assumption": conclusions, pejorative force, and basis. Arrange things so that you are really testing for the basis type of assumptions.

Devising Your Own Open-ended Approaches

To obtain information on certain aspects of critical thinking, particularly on dispositions and the use of critical thinking in social contexts, multiple-choice tests are unsuitable. We have suggested four open-ended approaches which are useful for these purposes: short-answer critical thinking testing, using argumentative essays, interviewing students as they work on problems, and carefully monitoring classroom discussions. Since only one approach of this sort is commercially available—The Ennis-Weir test—many of you will have to devise your own approach for your needs. To do this better, we suggested the following broad guidelines:

1. Pilot your evaluation with a sample of students to make sure that it provides an interesting context as the basis of the reasoning task.

2. In your pilot test, try to be sure that students understand the task or the questions in the way intended.

3. As part of the task, seek justification from students for what they say and write.

4. Be generous in interpreting students' responses.

5. When grading students' responses, distinguish the truth of what they say from its relevance to the task as you described it.

6. Look for patterns of strengths and weaknesses within individual student's responses and in responses from all students.

7. Try to infer the presence and absence of critical thinking dispositions from what students say or write and from what they do not say or write, and make notes on your inferences and the evidence for them.

Using Quality Information

Even high quality information on students' critical thinking can be used poorly. For example, quality information which focuses on a narrow aspect of critical thinking or which uses but one technique for gathering information should probably not be used for making important diagnostic and remediation decisions about particular individuals. A wide variety of information on several aspects of critical thinking would be more appropriate for this purpose. When the concern of the evaluation is to make decisions about the effectiveness of teachers, programs, or schools, then the highest quality information will be jeopardized unless sound experimental design is followed. Such design entails ensuring the treatment is implemented properly, collecting the required sort of comparative information, and ensuring that extraneous student-related, classroom-related, and teacher-related factors are controlled. The aim is to rule out plausible, competing interpretations of the information.

Concluding Remarks

The guidelines discussed in this book and briefly summarized in this chapter require judicious application by people with knowledge of education, critical thinking, and educational evaluation. There are no formulas to follow which can replace the knowledgeable and careful application of general principles. The most important principle to follow in evaluating students' critical thinking is that the evaluation itself should conform to the standards of critical thought.

APPENDIX:
TOPICS FOR EVALUATING
CRITICAL THINKING ABILITIES
(ELABORATED VERSION)

Elementary Clarification

1. Focusing on a question
   a. Identifying or formulating a question
   b. Identifying or formulating criteria for judging possible answers
   c. Keeping the situation in mind
2. Analyzing arguments
   a. Identifying conclusions
   b. Identifying stated reasons
   c. Identifying unstated reasons
   d. Seeing similarities and differences
   e. Identifying and handling irrelevance
   f. Seeing the structure of an argument
   g. Summarizing
3. Asking and answering questions of clarification and challenge; for example,
   a. Why?
   b. What is your main point?
   c. What do you mean by — — — — — — —?
   d. What would be an example?
   e. What would not be an example, though close to being one?

    f.   How does that case, which you seem to be offering as a counterexample, apply to this situation?

    g.   What difference does it make?

    h.   What are the facts?

    i.   Is this what you are saying, "– – – – – – –"?

    j.   Would you say more about that?

Basic Support

4.   Judging the credibility of a source—criteria for:

    a.   Expertise

    b.   Conflict of interest

    c.   Agreement with other sources

    d.   Reputation

    e.   Use of established procedures

    f.   Risk to reputation

    g.   Ability to give reasons

    h.   Careful habits

5.   Making and judging observations—important considerations in:

    a.   Characteristics of the observer; for example, alertness, normal senses, not overly emotional

    b.   Characteristics of the observation conditions; for example, quality of access, time to observe, opportunity to observe more than once, instrumentation

    c.   Characteristics of the observation statement; for example, closeness to time of observing, made by observer, based on reliable records

    d.   Topics "a" to "h" above, under "Judging the credibility of a source"

Inference

6. Making and judging deductions
   a. Class logic
   b. Conditional logic
   c. Interpretation of statements, including:
      1. Double negation
      2. Necessary and sufficient conditions
      3. Other logical words; for example, "only," "if," "if and only if," "or," "some," "unless," "not," "not both"

7. Making and judging inductions
   a. Generalizing—concerns in:
      1. Typicality of instances
      2. Limitations of coverage
      3. Sampling
      4. Tables and graphs
   b. Explaining and hypothesizing—criteria for:
      1. Explaining the evidence
      2. Consistency with known facts
      3. Alternative conclusions eliminated
      4. Plausibility
   c. Investigating
      1. Designing experiments, including planning that controls variables effectively
      2. Seeking evidence and counterevidence
      3. Seeking other possible conclusions

8. Making and judging value judgments—considerations in:
   a. Relevance of background facts
   b. Consequences of proposed action

    c.   Dependence on acceptable higher order value principles

    d.   Consideration and weighing of alternatives

Advanced Clarification

9.   Defining terms and judging definitions

    a.   Form of definition

       1.   Synonym

       2.   Classification

       3.   Range

       4.   Equivalent expression

       5.   Operational

       6.   Example-nonexample

    b.   Definitional strategy

       1.   Acts of defining

          a.   Reporting a meaning

          b.   Stipulating a meaning

          c.   Expressing a position on an issue

       2.   Identifying and handling equivocation

          a.   Paying attention to the context

          b.   Formulating an appropriate response

10.   Identifying assumptions

    a.   Unstated assumptions

    b.   Needed assumptions

Strategies and Tactics

11. Deciding on an action

    a.   Defining the problem

    b.   Selecting criteria to judge possible solutions

    c.   Formulating alternative solutions

     d.   Tentatively deciding what to do

     e.   Reviewing, taking into account the total situation, and deciding

     f.   Monitoring the decision-making process

12. Interacting with others

     a.   Employing and reacting to fallacy labels; for example, "Circularity," "Appeal to authority," "Ad hominem," "Equivocation," "Straw person"

     b.   Using rhetorical strategies

     c.   Presenting a position to a particular audience

GLOSSARY

Ability

To say that someone has an ability is to say that the person can do or has the power to do something. People can have abilities which they do not use, either because they do not think to use them or because they do not choose to. (Compare *Disposition.*)

Aspect-specific Test

An aspect-specific critical thinking test is one that focuses on a single aspect of critical thinking, such as ability to identify assumptions, ability to judge the credibility of sources, inductive reasoning ability, or ability in defining. (Compare *Comprehensive Test.*)

Comprehensive Test

A critical thinking test is comprehensive to the degree that it includes tasks on each of the five broad areas of critical thinking: clarity-related abilities, inference-related abilities, basic-support-related abilities, strategies and tactics, and dispositions. (Compare *Aspect-specific Test.*)

Construct

A construct is a postulated trait of human beings, such as critical thinking ability, intelligence, and anxiety. Constructs are thought to underlie performance and to explain its occurrence.

Criterion-referencing

In criterion-referenced testing, students' scores are compared to a standard of satisfactory performance which has been set in advance. (Compare *Norm-referencing*.)

Critical Thinking

The central idea of critical thinking is reasonable and reflective thinking that is focused upon deciding what to believe or do. So conceived, thinking critically requires abilities, strategies and tactics, and dispositions.

Deduction

Deduction is a type of inference. (See *Inference*.) Deductive inference arrives at conclusions that follow necessarily from the reasons given. Accepting the reasons means that the conclusion must be accepted. (Compare *Induction*.)

Deductive Validity

Deductive validity refers to the logical strength of reasoning. To say that some reasoning is deductively valid is to say that it would be inconsistent to accept the premises of the reasoning and not to accept the conclusion. Deductive validity does not refer to the truth of the premises or the conclusion. (Compare *Validity*.)

Disposition

Dispositions motivate and justify the use of abilities and define frames of mind. To say that someone has a disposition to use an ability is to say that the person uses the ability when it is appropriate to do so. Dispositions such as open-mindedness, tentativeness, and inquisitiveness define frames of mind. (Compare *Ability*.)

Evaluation

In the context of this book, evaluation involves gathering information on students' critical thinking and using that information to make value judgments about the students themselves, about teachers, teaching methods, instructional programs, etc. Evaluation is different from testing, because testing is just one way to gather information for use in making an evaluation.

General-knowledge Test

A general-knowledge critical thinking test is one that calls for no advanced knowledge in any particular discipline or school subject. (Compare *Subject-specific Test.*)

Induction

Induction is a type of inference. (See *Inference.*) Inductive inference arrives at conclusions that are explanations or generalizations. These conclusions go beyond the reasons or evidence offered in their support. (Compare *Deduction.*)

Inference

Inference is the process of reaching conclusions based upon reasons.

Norm-referencing

In norm-referenced testing, students' scores are interpreted by determining where they fall compared to other students' scores. (Compare *Criterion-referencing.*)

Open-ended Test

An open-ended critical thinking test is one in which examinees do more than choose among alternatives. They must supply answers ranging from one word to long essays, and from written responses to actions in a situation.

Reliability

The reliability of a test in the technical, psychometric sense is the consistency of performance on the test from one taking of the test to another by the same individuals. Reliability in this technical sense is different from the everyday sense; in the everyday sense, to be reliable is to be trustworthy. (Compare *Validity*.)

Subject-specific Test

A subject-specific critical thinking test measures critical thinking in some particular school subject and calls for special knowledge of that subject. (Compare *General-knowledge Test*.)

Validity

The validity of a test is the degree to which scores on the test can be trusted to mean what they are purported to mean. (Compare *Reliability* and *Deductive Validity*.)

INDEX

Methods development, 171-172
Millman, Jason, 97
Moorburg letter, 2, 82
Multiple-choice items
    assumption-identification, 119
    credibility, 112
    deduction, 110
    elements of, 107
    guidelines for making, 179
    induction, 116
Multiple-choice justification
    controlling background beliefs by, 114, 118
    item independence and, 115
    leading examinees through, 115
Multiple-choice tests
    adapting for oral administration, 162
    advantages of, 28
    compared to constructed-response tests, 30-31, 81-82, 129
    compared to monitoring discussions, 154
    compared to open-ended tests, 129
    disadvantages of, 29
    disposition testing and, 30
    format of, 28
    improving validity of, 29
    individual testing with, 103
    making, 101, 179-180
    preparing students for, 102-103
    reliability of, 28
    roles of, 29
    thinking processes hidden by, 29
New Jersey Test of Reasoning Skills, 94, 98, 123
    reliability and validity of, 75
    uses of, 73
Noncomparative-judgment approach, 110, 113, 179
    advantages of, 111
Norm-referenced testing, 104
Norris, Stephen P., 26, 53, 99, 158
O'Reilly, Kevin, 151, 168
Observation, direct classroom
    advantages of, 32